CONFERENCE ON THE TEACHING OF FOREIGN LANGUAGES

THE
FRIENDLY
CONFERENCE!

Defining the Essentials for the Foreign Language Classroom

Selected Papers from the 1989
Central States Conference

Edited by

Dave McAlpine

Morningside College, Sioux City, Iowa

Coeditors

Bette LeFeber Ervin
Ohio Dominican College, Columbus, Ohio

Diane Ging
Columbus Public Schools, Columbus, Ohio

National Textbook Company
a division of NTC *Publishing Group* • Lincolnwood, Illinois USA

Published by National Textbook Company, a division of NTC Publishing Group.
© 1989 by NTC Publishing Group, 4255 West Touhy Avenue,
Lincolnwood (Chicago), Illinois 60646-1975 U.S.A.

Preface

As the Central States Conference meets this year in Nashville, we note that this year, our twenty-first annual gathering, is mindful of the rapidly approaching 21st century and the challenges it will surely bring to the peoples of the world to communicate more effectively. No less is our challenge to find new and better ways to facilitate communication through research and understanding of how peoples of diverse cultures can more effectively relate to one another.

The subthemes of this year's conference attempt to address areas of major concern and interest to foreign language teachers: (1) political action, (2) foreign language and careers, (3) curricula for proficiency, (4) testing, (5) teaching for production, (6) teaching for comprehension, (7) FLES/FLEX/immersion, (8) modern technology, (9) culture, and (10) education/certification for the 1990s. Combined, they constitute the "TENN-ESSEntials" of foreign language instruction. Individually, many are areas of challenge that have been around for years—which in itself tells us the job is not finished. Others are new horizons to conquer.

Modern technology holds much promise for the future, and the age of computers is well entrenched in the language-teaching profession. The student of tomorrow (today?) will surely be lost without a mastery of basic computer skills around which the classroom of tomorrow will be organized.

Striving for proficiency in communicative skills will remain a major priority and to that end many sessions this year have been dedicated.

The conference participants this year were challenged to think and act globally in a multitude of domains by the keynote speakers, Mary Hatwood Futrell, president of the National Education Association, and Protase Woodford of the Educational Testing Service.

The conference, through its 101 sessions and 21 workshops, was designed to bring a variety of challenges to the attendees and to provide a forum for the exchange of theoretical and practical information that could be taken back to the classroom on Monday morning and put to immediate use. If but a portion of those challenges were met, we must consider that this conference, as those that have preceded it, has been a success.

William N. Hatfield
1989 Program Chair

Contents

Introduction

Dave McAlpine
Morningside College, Sioux City, Iowa

How does one define the essentials for today's foreign language class-room? Who is to say that political action, career opportunities, curricula for proficiency, or testing procedures are more important than the profession's interest in FLES, technology, or culture? Not many among us would be willing to list but ten essentials for the language classroom of the 1990s. Had a clever punster not been at work, the "TENN-ESSEntials" of the 1989 Central States Conference theme could have easily been stretched to fifteen or twenty. Now that our profession has found support and made allies on many fronts, the challenge to define the essentials is upon us. This volume of the Central States Conference *Report* represents only eleven of the many essential elements believed important by foreign language professionals.

June K. Phillips's lead article is most closely related to this volume's title and to the conference theme. Phillips suggests an action agenda—one that moves us beyond the talk stage. She posits five principles conducive to proficiency development and encourages us to put these principles into action.

Improving listening comprehension of the intermediate foreign language student is the subject of Tracy David Terrell's article. Terrell relates how a video course can provide students, without experience living in the target language culture, the comprehensible input necessary to move them from an intermediate level to an advanced level in listening comprehension.

Julie A. Storme and H. Jay Siskin focus their article on developing reading skills to assist students in overcoming the difficult and often discouraging process of reading literature. The authors present strategies for predicting, intensive reading, extensive reading, verification, and finally the transition to reading.

"Global Education in the Language Classroom: The African Connection" by Millie Park Mellgren encourages foreign language teachers not to treat the culture of their subject matter in isolation. The culture of the language we teach is a significant part of a global society and foreign language teachers can make a significant difference in raising the awareness of the interdependence of the peoples and cultures of the world.

Continuing the theme of culture begun by Mellgren, Kathleen G. Boykin explores that essential area of the curriculum by adding a variety of student-centered activities to the traditional history-culture course. She advocates the use of videos, realia, newspapers, magazines, and other authentic materials as ways to make the course both exciting and useful for today's students.

Diane W. Birckbichler encourages us to establish course goals and then examine the contribution of classroom activities, materials, and techniques to these goals. In her article, "Classroom Activities: A Task-Analysis Approach," she suggests that a methodological approach may pose problems and instead presents the alternative of the task analysis, in which teachers examine dimensions of classroom tasks, their characteristics, and their outcomes.

One real essential in the foreign language classroom is the textbook. Alan Garfinkel and Mary Beth Berghian underscore the cover-the-textbook syndrome so prevalent in our profession. In their timely article, "You and Your Textbook: Legal Separation—Not a Divorce," they conclude that the textbook should be our guide rather than a list of things to do.

Another growing area in the foreign language profession that, undoubtedly, will become a classroom essential is the use of feature films and videos. Tom Carr suggests a range of approaches for their use in the French culture class.

"Crossing the Rubicon: Bridging the Gap between 'Grammar' and 'Literature' in the Intermediate Latin Course" by Jeffrey L. Buller makes a case for the continued use of Caesar's *Gallic Wars* in today's Latin classroom.

As mainstreaming of students with specific learning difficulties becomes more common in the foreign language classroom, teachers will need to have methodologies in hand that help them help these students be successful in foreign language learning. Bettye J. Myer, Leonore Ganschow, Richard Sparks, and Sylvia Kenneweg discuss the Orton-Gillingham method of teaching the decoding and encoding of written language and how that method may be applied in the second language classroom.

This year's volume concludes with Nicole Fouletier-Smith's article on implementing "learning cycles" in a civilization course. She discusses the ADAPT Program of exploration, invention, and application as it applies to the study of culture.

The process of defining the essentials for the foreign language classroom is a difficult one. The articles included here have only begun to address this question. As we continue to define the essentials, let us not forget to include the two most important ones—the student and the teacher.

Acknowledgments

Thanks are due to the following professionals who evaluated the many papers submitted to this year's volume of the Central States Conference *Report*: Carolyn Andrade, Cincinnati Public Schools; Marjorie Artzer, Northwestern High School, Cincinnati, Ohio; Rosemarie Benya, East Central University, Ada, Oklahoma; Karen Hardy Cárdenas, The University of South Dakota, Vermillion, South Dakota; Walter Chatfield, Iowa State University, Ames, Iowa; Helena Anderson Curtain, Milwaukee Public Schools; Audrey L. Heining-Boyton, University of North Carolina, Chapel Hill, North Carolina; Robert Hawkins, Upper Arlington High School, Columbus, Ohio; Jan Herrera, Colorado Department of Education, Thornton, Colorado; Diane Kessler, College of St. Scholastica, Duluth, Minnesota; Katherine C. Kurk, Northern Kentucky University, Highland Heights, Kentucky; Francis Lide, Michigan Technological University, Houghton, Michigan; Mary Sula Linney, Iowa Central Community College, Fort Dodge, Iowa; Martha Nyikos, Indiana University, Bloomington, Indiana; Michael D. Oates, The University of Northern Iowa, Cedar Falls, Iowa; Ruben Peterson, Central College, Pella, Iowa; Carol Ragan, Morningside College, Sioux City, Iowa; JoAnn Recker, Xavier University, Cincinnati, Ohio; Virginia Senor, Shaw High School, East Cleveland, Ohio; Karen Soukup, University of Nebraska at Omaha; Alice Strange, Southeast Missouri State University, Cape Girardeau, Missouri; Toni Theisen, Walt Clark Junior High School, Loveland, Colorado; Marie Trayer, Millard South High School, Omaha, Nebraska; Ronald W. Walker, Colorado State University, Fort Collins, Colorado.

The editor is particularly grateful for the excellent help of his two coeditors, who carried out their responsibilities so competently and efficiently. Bette Ervin evaluated and provided editorial comments for each article submitted and for those included in this volume. In addition to coordinating the work of the twenty-four readers listed above, Diane Ging evaluated and edited all the submitted articles.

The editor is also indebted to Norma May of the Foreign Language Department of Morningside College for her computer preparation of the final manuscript and to Shellie Athey of the same department, who compiled the ratings of the evaluators.

1
From Talk to Action: An Essential for Curricular Change

June K. Phillips
Tennessee Foreign Language Institute, Nashville

As the last decade of this century greets us, we might look carefully at the *essence* of foreign language education. The essential element is change, more specifically curricular change in a variety of dimensions.

Heading the list of essentials is **political action**, usually an agent for change, sometimes a means of preserving the status quo. **Foreign language and careers**, if this pairing is to reach beyond teaching as a profession, require a degree of curricular change and innovation that does more than pay lip service to **curricula for proficiency. Testing** has to undergo change if evaluation is to align itself more suitably with **teaching for production** and **teaching for comprehension.** Multiple changes are occurring in **FLES/FLEX/immersion** programs in elementary schools. **Modern technology** brings change by providing access to contemporary language and **culture.** Yet all is for naught if we fail to meet the challenge of **education/certification for the 1990s.**

This article explores, not the ten essentials mentioned above, but the change element embedded in some of them; and it challenges the profession to move forward on an action agenda. None of the themes is new; all have been around for some time. Talk has been prolific. These themes dominate program presentations at conferences or workshops and titles of journal articles and book chapters. Yet, in many instances, they remain at the level of talk, and we approach the 21st century having only timidly and sporadically initiated the curricular changes identified as essential. Time is of the essence; first graders who entered school in September 1988 will graduate in the year 2000. If their foreign language experience is to prepare them better for the multilingual world we talk about, then action must occur: (1) to achieve an articulated K–life curriculum; (2) to make the content of the second language classroom match the content of messages conveyed and messages received; and (3) to implement successful strategies for teaching and for learning in classrooms.

The Curriculum:
For Proficiency, for Articulation, for Meaningful Content

A new generation of curriculum guides has arisen. No longer presuming to produce near-native speakers in two years, curriculum developers now struggle to find more positive ways of saying "barely intelligible" or "most utterances contain fractured syntax." In spite of arguments over supposed differences between communicative competence and proficiency, the impact of a communicative orientation to language teaching has been significant. More realistic objectives have been set, they are phrased in measurable terms, they are performance descriptions, and they address global competencies rather than short-term discrete-point coverage. Secondary school curriculum guides in most states reflect the influence of documents such as the ACTFL Proficiency Guidelines (1) or the College Board's (4) academic competencies. At the college level, when revision of either basic or advanced sequences has occurred, proficiency has been an organizing principle. (See Heilenman and Kaplan, 7; James, 8.)

Proficiency is neither a new word nor a new concept. Teachers have always wanted students to attain a usable level of skill. While a communicative goal always existed, teaching time was targeted on language forms. The hope seemed to be that "parole" would be achieved from lessons based on "langue."

The proficiency descriptions have offered clearer insights into the reality of students' performances as they advance through a continuum of language tasks. While the descriptions have not been generated by a theory of language acquisition, neither are they the figment of someone's imagination. The derivation of the government version was based upon actual speech samples analyzed for the language tasks, wherein content was controlled by speakers. The resulting performance clusters were subsequently described in terms of function, content, and accuracy.

Over the past years, the profession has experimented with adapted descriptions as evaluation measures for speaking and as guidelines for curriculum. The movement has not been without controversy, yet the development of a curriculum more in touch with the communicative goals espoused is gaining momentum. This has occurred partly because the Oral Proficiency Interview has served as a viable means of assessing speaking across programs and levels, and partly because the emphasis on outcomes is descriptive of performance, not prescriptive of method or approach (Liskin-Gasparro, 10; Lowe, 11).

From Talk about Proficiency to Action

Proficiency, the label, has been attached to just about everything (as demonstrated by the educator who claimed to practice proficiency because his students were proficient at pattern drills). Distinguishing between talk and action, however, is not always easy. The talk has moved to action in terms of statements of objectives and subsequent curricular design (Medley, 12; Phillips, 15). Most curricular revision in the schools and in higher education includes realistic outcome statements in terms of real-world performance. For example, Tennessee's state curriculum guide reminds teachers of outcome by printing the relevant College Board competency at the bottom of each page. The majority of today's state and district guides reflect the language of the ACTFL guidelines. Textbooks, too, at all levels outdo one another in claiming to develop proficiency better, faster, and with less pain than the competition. After having set objectives, however, many curriculum guides and tables of contents in textbooks stop at the talk stage. The guide often continues to list grammatical coverage and vocabulary much as it always did; the texts do likewise. The link between the objectives as stated and the language as studied remains far apart. Communicative activities still carry the tag "Optional" in the margin; and in the classroom, the objective of having students demonstrate their ability "to talk about self and interests" soon becomes lost in daily concerns with forms, rules, and exceptions.

The Proficiency Syllabus

An action agenda that matches the talk will occur when the Latin-derived grammatical syllabus gives way to one that more closely resembles the order in which language is logically acquired, when message achieves equal status with form. The realization that grammar has overwhelmed everything else in the classroom has not transferred to lessening its dominance nor to identifying the level and tasks for which greater degrees of grammatical accuracy should be sought.

Proficiency is compatible with the teaching of grammar, with achievement testing, with pronunciation. It does not deny the value of the tools; they are necessary but not sufficient. The caution is that language teaching still clings to all the pieces even as it complains about the overload in coverage. Unfortunately, the pieces are easy to teach, easy to learn. Memorizing dialogs is simpler than creating thoughts with language. It takes less effort to teach students to act out a skit to perform on Parents' Night than to teach them to help mom or dad order a meal on a summer vacation, or to assist a new foreign neighbor learn the ropes of daily life in the "good ole U.S.A."

Proficiency goals have simply been attached to the old curriculum or text sequence. The challenge to review traditional instructional content in terms of desired performances remains, and the process may benefit from a clean start by placing the objectives on blank paper and deriving the classroom content from the language, culture, communication, and discourse strategies needed to accomplish the tasks.

The Oral Proficiency Interview has been particularly enlightening in demonstrating that input does not equal output. Teachers who have either observed or conducted interviews are often startled, and sometimes appalled, at seeing their own students converse. Well aware of the specific points of grammar taught, practiced, and tested (therefore learned), they find that the same students who completed exercises successfully in past, future, and conditional speak in what can only be described as the timeless present.

Input does not equal output, and neither does performance on a discrete point test equate with an authentic conversation that removes the obvious classroom cues. The language-learning process is not as neat as a verb paradigm or the rule for agreement of the past participle. The rate at which language is internalized and then produced differs greatly from one student to another, and that variation arises from a complex interaction of cognitive, affective, and personality factors that still need to be investigated.

The Time/Aptitude Dimension

Another action point for a truly proficiency-oriented curriculum relates to the factor of time. Even before proficiency, in the days when individualized instruction was more widely practiced, the time/aptitude dimension received much attention. Carroll's (3) model of school learning with its emphasis on time needed, time willing to spend, time allowed, is no less valid for communicative approaches than it was for previous methods. Yet movement away from "seat time" requirements seldom occurs, and those who have really dared to adopt proficiency requirements remain small in number (Freed, 5; Schulz, 17). The proficiency-based objectives add a touch of realism to foreign language instruction, and their existence plays a role in the expanded student body now enrolling in language classes. As states and communities institute new language requirements based upon the belief that all students can learn language within real-world contexts, time will remain a critical factor. Students can achieve the outcomes built into curricular mandates; however, some need more time to do so. If the competencies are legitimate, if they truly prepare students for academic success or competitiveness in a global economy, then learners should be granted the time they need to reach those objectives. When do we act upon our talk? When do we give supremacy to the goal by awarding the credit with performance, not years?

Making Articulation Happen

Articulation, another professional priority which continues to evade action, like proficiency, receives headline attention at conferences and in journals. Why this historic lack of articulation as evidenced by the number of individuals who report "Oh, I studied four years of French (German, Spanish): of course, three were French (German, Spanish) I"? Absence of articulation arises in part from differences in goals at various levels of instruction, yet diversity of goals is not in itself negative. In fact, elementary, secondary, and university programs should reflect different objectives, but different should not mean incompatible nor should it result in recycled learners. Our failure to implement articulated sequences prohibits students from growing in the language tasks they can perform, the content/contexts in which they can function, and the accuracy with which they use another language.

Presently, students continue to be recycled and awarded credit for repeated skills and redundant knowledge. We can no longer operate in an environment where the university values students who can recite the litanies of language rules and follow grammatical explanations in the target language and where feeder schools stress the oral skills and tolerance for error advocated by their curricular mandates. Neither can secondary schools ignore the oral skills students acquire in elementary or middle schools by placing them in classes with raw beginners and a first-year text because only the grammar really counts in a serious program. Moving beyond talk about articulation to making it happen requires: (1) dialog and commitment to articulate; and (2) design, implementation, and monitoring to ensure it.

For a profession so enraptured by dialogs, how strange it is that we experience so much difficulty when the goal is creative interchange among colleagues rather than memorized utterances among students. The dialog requires listening as well as speaking and a predilection for higher-level thinking and discourse (e.g., hypothesizing, persuading, convincing, solving problems). The talk stage has generated models; the time is right for teachers of foreign language at all levels to act to make change happen. Lange (9) describes vertical and horizontal models of articulation before proposing a broader definition based upon the multiple syllabi that constitute the second language curriculum: the general language syllabus, the linguistic syllabus, the communicative syllabus, and the cultural syllabus. If teachers would actually identify the outcomes that students achieve from their courses in these syllabi, then subsequent levels could build upon those competencies.

The Problem of Articulation

The bottom line demands that we do a better job of articulation; otherwise the public support now enjoyed will just as quickly disappear. The enthusiasm about earlier language study and about requirements for college admission will wane with the realization that elementary students exit programs being able to name common items and converse about family, pastimes, and interests; four years later they exit high school being able to do the same things and after two more years of Language I and II, the story is much the same. Of course, they could not advance more than that because their verb forms remained messy when they took the placement test. Try selling that to the public!

Initiating and maintaining the dialog has been facilitated through the growth of support systems such as Academic Alliances, school/college collaboratives, and professional organizations that cross educational levels. Once dialog has been established, there must be a mutual commitment to build upon what is. Proficiency descriptions can be useful in identifying the global tasks students have learned to perform. Those performances probably endure over a longer time (but research on retention on this measure is needed), a summer hiatus for example, than do the discrete points of grammar that form the basis for most placement testing. Beyond the articulation point between secondary and higher education, some of the more salient implications from proficiency-oriented approaches concern the concept of a spiraled curriculum in which students gain conceptual, partial, full control of language forms and tasks through a series of developmental passes (Medley, 12). The lockstep aspect of language learning has been cemented in place for far too long. No matter how much drill or practice, teaching past tense to supposed mastery at a given point, i.e., second semester, does not mean the student can use it for a variety of tasks. Providing opportunities for past narration in many contexts for many years builds control of form, but it remains subservient to message and meaning.

Alleviating the articulation problem would contribute toward achieving the lifelong language learner talked about, or at least thought about, in rationales for foreign language study. Even in the literature for school learners, the preponderance of research studies and of shared activities concentrates on beginning to intermediate stages. Much less information exists on advanced learners and next to nothing on adults seeking to maintain functional levels of language or to grow in them. In the established business and government communities, interest centers upon informal programs where people can hear the language and speak it with appropriate feedback or illumination. Credits carry no value, nor does classroom paraphernalia such as homework, esoteric explanations, or mechanical exercises. Diagnosis and needs assessment are the key factors to this kind of individual articulation—determining what the person can now do with language and expanding the tasks, content, and accuracy to assure progress or perhaps only maintenance.

Curricular Change through Content

As the content of instruction shifts toward performance, the "can do" statements developed in the communicative curriculum gain influence over both planned and spontaneous classroom activities. No single topic outranks "communicative activities" in popularity at conferences and in the literature. Yet classroom observations and teachers' confessions during question-and-answer sessions reveal that talk overrules action on the daily scene. Whether from fear of insufficiently attending to grammar (so students score well on standardized tests and in college) or from uneasiness about controlling a class where students really express themselves, the classroom balance tilts heavily toward the mechanical exercise and convergent response. Until significant numbers of teachers cease believing that the subsets of language, that is the phonology, the grammar, the vocabulary, are the ends as well as the means, action to shift instructional practice toward the communicative lags behind the talk. Action means setting an agenda that creates, first and foremost, opportunities for practice in meaningful contexts. As teachers gain experience with practice that binds form and meaning, stronger will be the propensity to abandon, at long last, much of the unnecessary mechanistic drill.

Years ago, it was claimed that second language study was a content-free discipline, not a contentless one (Phillips, 14). In that sense, the class draws upon a wide array of personal, cultural, social, global, or other curricular content—it simply works with that content in another language. Elementary programs are opting for content-based instruction in significant numbers over "traditional" FLES. Some innovative college programs have experimented with teaching courses from other disciplines in a foreign language (e.g., Earlham College, IN; Boston College, MA). Discipline-based courses in a foreign language make the link with careers a reality by permitting students to study their content in another language. Nonetheless, a glance at lesson plans for most language classes reveals almost total concentration on grammar points and vocabulary categories as exemplified by "Tuesday: Reflexive verbs and daily routines."

Changing the action in the classroom means that the teacher will question, constantly and consistently, the direction of exercises and the fit with the overall objective of the unit. Whenever that inquiry results in mechanistic, forced, noncommunicative responses that cannot be tied to a potential real-world use, the contribution of the activity should be reassessed. Teachers must become better analyzers of exercises in an effort toward improving the match between expected outcomes and language actually generated. Unless manipulation can be justified by being initial practice or perhaps remedial (but even there is not meaningfulness equally desirable?), a means of contextualization or a performance parallel should be sought. The rationale for this action does not relate to any student inability to produce language forms; they can very successfully spout paradigms or recite rules. Being able to talk about or read about or hear about content that matters is more challenging.

If we act on implementing more functional objectives, texts will become guides to content, not content themselves. Proficiency guidelines and curricula that reflect that orientation facilitate the process. For example, Novice/Intermediate level speakers benefit from a personalized vocabulary to a greater degree than previously. The text can set topic, establish tasks, and provide a resource list. Teacher alteration of, addition to, and subtraction from the text is necessary, for when students do "message work" they generally try to tell the truth.

One would be led to believe that all students in a language class come from families of doctors, lawyers, and teachers. Teachers conducting oral interviews realize how the content of the course has made a simple task (Tell me about your family) more complex for the student whose parent is a factory worker, miner, or supermarket cashier. For example, students from a neat nuclear family of father, mother, sister, brother enjoy a linguistic advantage over stepchildren or merged-family students, who no longer are minorities in our classrooms. Adult learners in college find that the text ignores their status and relegates them to being children of their parents rather than parents of their children. Set the task and derive the content from it—a simple formula that changes the action in the second language class.

The introduction of authentic materials into the classroom also heightens the degree of content other than language forms. Strategies for providing access to authentic materials appear abundantly in the literature (Byrnes, 2; Glisan, 6; Phillips; 16). Developing receptive skills with authentic materials is more challenging than permitting students to work with materials authored or edited for them. The problem with the latter is that they tend to be without significant or culturally appropriate content; the problem with authentic materials lies in degree of difficulty. Familiarizing students with the content of authentic texts through prelistening, prereading activities and similar strategies leads to successful comprehension. Skill and new knowledge in content areas are developed simultaneously. After the language course is over, students are more likely to remember the content of a video about meter maids in Paris or of a reading contrasting poverty and tourism in a Caribbean nation.

Individual Teachers Acting on Instructional Principles

Teaching changes ultimately occur at the classroom level with individual teachers assuming responsibility for instructional action and interaction with their learners. Omaggio (13, pp. 44–53) hypothesizes about the proficiency-oriented classroom and describes it as a place where

1. Opportunities must be provided for students to practice using language in a range of contexts likely to be encountered in the target culture
2. Opportunities should be provided for students to practice carrying out a range of functions (task universals) likely to be necessary in dealing with others in the target culture
3. There is a concern for the development of linguistic accuracy from the beginning of instruction
4. The methodologies respond to the affective needs of students as well as to their cognitive needs
5. The methodologies promote cultural understanding and prepare students to live more harmoniously in the target language community

Those hypotheses lay the groundwork for the activities and practices described in Omaggio's very popular methods text.

Classroom teachers can make the proficiency-oriented classroom a reality by adopting for themselves a few "guiding principles" for language learning and then adjust instructional approaches, materials, and learning activities so that they reflect those principles. The decision-making process becomes easier when a solid basis for action is established. Some materials creation will certainly be involved, but the greatest degree of change arises from a conscious choice of strategy premised upon what is known about proficiency levels and student performances within their ranges. That knowledge base determines how teachers focus instruction, how they carry out activities, and how they achieve the balance of getting and using skills.

Principles Conducive to Proficiency Development

The author posits here a set of principles that might serve as a "mindset" for the teacher interested in utilizing strategies conducive to proficiency development. They are not meant to be prescriptive, but suggestive. They are in a formative stage in the mind of the author and thus not comprehensive; they are personal and not a methodology for the profession. Teachers working toward the development of functional proficiency with their students will add their own guiding principles by deriving them from their experience with learners and making them compatible with their teaching strengths.

Principle 1.   Derive the content of the classroom from the functions and context of proficiency descriptions. That means that the end performances sought influence most strongly what is taught in the classroom. Furthermore, student time will be spent as much as possible on using and understanding language that conveys real-world messages. Exercises will be upgraded so that they build upon the potential for communication if not the immediacy of it. Often this only involves teacher intervention to redirect exercises, to adjust formats; it rarely means rewriting the text or abandoning it.

Principle 2.   Aim for truth telling and personalization to the greatest extent possible. The simple adjustment of "answer as you would in real life" affects significantly the cued-response format of "What did you do Saturday night? Answer: (go to the movies)." If learners operate from a premise of communication from the beginning, they will gain confidence by practicing the actual language forms most likely to express individual meanings, ideas, opinions. Content articulation occurs naturally as the task generates different responses from a ten-year-old, a teenager, a college student, an adult businessperson.

Principle3.   Seek comprehensible input from authentic listening and reading materials. Authentic materials, as mentioned, can be used at earlier stages by providing students access through techniques to familiarize them with the content and to train them in the strategies that lead to comprehension. By placing receptive materials at a "challenge" stage, productive activities may be developed from them. Student outcomes include new knowledge and enriched matter for speaking or writing.

Principle 4.   Spiral the grammar to achieve conceptual, partial, and full control. Buying into this concept means relinquishing obedience to a lifelong loyalty to the organization of the grammar syllabus from simple to complex and instead choosing one based upon language purpose, function, task, or any other real-world usage factor. Further work is needed to determine the structural control that will be appropriate and realistic for given levels of instruction.

Principle 5.   Increase the amount of student-to-student interactions in the classroom. The role of teachers shifts from center-stage performer to that of a true facilitator, stage manager, or director. Paired exercises and small-group activities assume more importance in the class. This change affects students in their roles as well as teachers. Students become full partners in the learning experience. They must be taught to try, to venture, to cope, to create—and they must be willing to take risks, to be wrong or misunderstood at times. In the past, it was much easier to memorize than to think, to recite verbatim than to convey new thoughts.

Conclusion

The principles enumerated here seek to support the talk-to-action agenda suggested in this article. Curriculum that proposes communicative goals, curriculum that aims at an articulated language experience, curriculum that spawns practices to promote language proficiency—this kind of curriculum must move beyond the talk stage. As the 21st century approaches, action should be the issue, and action means doing, implementing, researching, evaluating, and changing again if warranted. Let us replace the rigor of a methodology with the responsibility for wise decision making and let this all lead to a language learner capable of communicating in another language; let us eliminate a future where adults reminisce about their school experiences by equating years of language studied with lack of language learned.

References

1. *ACTFL Proficiency Guidelines*. Hastings-on-Hudson, NY: ACTFL Materials Center, 1985.
2. Byrnes, Heidi. "Teaching toward Proficiency: The Receptive Skills," pp. 77–107 in Alice C. Omaggio, ed., *Proficiency, Curriculum, Articulation: The Ties That Bind*. Middlebury, VT: Northeast Conference, 1985.
3. Carroll, John B. "A Model of School Learning." *Teachers College Record* 64 (1963):723–33.
4. College Board. *Academic Preparation in Foreign Language: Teaching for Transition from High School to College*. New York: College Entrance Examination Board, 1986.
5. Freed, Barbara. "Preliminary Impressions of the Effects of a Proficiency-Based Language Requirement." *Foreign Language Annals* 20 (1987):139–46.
6. Glisan, Eileen W. "A Plan for Teaching Listening Comprehension: Adaptation of an Instructional Reading Model." *Foreign Language Annals* 21 (1988):9–16.
7. Heilenman, Laura, and Isabelle Kaplan. "Proficiency in Practice: The Foreign Language Curriculum," pp. 55–78 in Charles J. James, ed., *Foreign Language Proficiency in the Classroom and Beyond*. ACTFL Foreign Language Education Series. Lincolnwood, IL: National Textbook Company, 1985.

8. James, Dorothy. "Toward Realistic Objectives in Foreign Language Teaching." *ADFL Bulletin* 16:2 (1985):9–12.
9. Lange, Dale. "Articulation: A Resolvable Problem?" pp. 11–31 in John P. Lalande II, ed., *Shaping the Future of Foreign Language Education: FLES, Articulation, and Proficiency.* Report of the Central States Conference on the Teaching of Foreign Languages. Lincolnwood, IL: National Textbook Company, 1988.
10. Liskin-Gasparro, Judith E. "The ACTFL Proficiency Guidelines: A Historical Perspective," pp. 11–42 in Theodore V. Higgs, ed., *Teaching for Proficiency, the Organizing Principle.* ACTFL Foreign Language Education Series. Lincolnwood, IL: National Textbook Company, 1984.
11. Lowe, Pardee. "The ILR Proficiency Scale as a Synthesizing Research Principle: The View from the Mountain," pp. 9–53 in Charles J. James, ed., *Foreign Language Proficiency in the Classroom and Beyond.* ACTFL Foreign Language Education Series. Lincolnwood, IL: National Textbook Company, 1985.
12. Medley, Frank, Jr. "Designing the Proficiency-Based Curriculum," pp. 13–40 in Alice C. Omaggio, ed., *Proficiency, Curriculum, Articulation: The Ties That Bind.* Middlebury, VT: Northeast Conference, 1985.
13. Omaggio, Alice C. *Teaching Language in Context: Proficiency-Oriented Instruction.* Boston: Heinle & Heinle, 1986.
14. Phillips, June K. "Introduction: Language in the Link," pp. 1–6 in June K. Phillips, ed., *The Language Connection: From the Classroom to the World.* ACTFL Foreign Language Education Series. Lincolnwood, IL: National Textbook Company, 1977.
15. _____. "Outcomes and Expectancies in a Proficiency-Oriented Program Toward Realistic Objectives." *ADFL Bulletin* 16:3 (1985):9–12.
16. _____. "Practical Implications of Recent Research in Reading." *Foreign Language Annals* 17 (1984):285–96.
17. Schulz, Renate. "Proficiency-Based Foreign Language Requirements: A Plan for Action." *ADFL Bulletin* 19:2 (1988):24–28.

2
Comprehensible Input for Intermediate Foreign Language Students via Video

Tracy David Terrell
University of California, San Diego

Improving listening comprehension of the intermediate student was the focus of an experimental Spanish course at the University of California, San Diego campus. The aim of the course was to improve the abilities of English-speaking intermediate students to understand the Spanish of the broadcast media. The course and its outcome are described in some detail with the hope that others will experiment with similar courses. Intermediate courses in oral comprehension hold interest for two reasons: (1) current acquisition research and theory accords primary importance to oral comprehension in the acquisition process, and (2) students in the course reported gains in their confidence to interact with native speakers.

One of the commonly accepted goals for foreign language students is the ability to comprehend the target language when it is spoken by native speakers in a normal conversational context. Comprehension of oral language was not a priority for teachers and students of a foreign language in earlier periods of public school education. Traditionally in U.S. public education the ability to read and translate was emphasized as the most important objective of foreign language study. The audiolingual "revolution" of the 50s and 60s emphasized four language skills: listening, speaking, reading, and writing. This new emphasis on oral skills, in conjunction with advances in technology that resulted in language labs, brought about increases in comprehension skills. However, the increases were not great, most likely because language-lab material focused on production—on the practice of dialogs and pattern drills. In retrospect this was a strange development, since audio equipment is clearly more suited to the development of listening than speaking skills. Even today, most audio programs for the language lab do not concentrate on oral comprehension.

On one hand, it must be admitted that it is not easy to provide the sort of input in the classroom or in the language lab that would be necessary to develop intermediate or advanced levels of oral comprehension skills. Natural language learners, who are immersed in the target language culture on a daily basis, typically are able to understand more complex language than they can speak. On the other hand, classroom-trained students have quite low levels of comprehension. Typically they are able to initiate a conversation, but frequently they are unable to understand the native speaker's response.

One problem in advancing comprehension skills arises from the nature of classroom discourse itself: classroom interaction is in fact simpler than discourse outside the classroom. Classroom language is likely to be slower, includes familiar topics, and very often consists of group discussion without the requirements of a normal one-on-one interchange of normal dialog. In addition, only rarely do students have to comprehend dialog between native speakers—a very common situation in the target culture.

It is not that comprehension skills gained from listening to teacher input are without value, but rather that they are different from listening skills acquired by native speakers and "natural" second language learners by virtue of their being exposed to a wider range of listening contexts. Here are some common listening skills utilized by natural learners daily: participating in extended one-on-one dialog, listening to others talking, listening to the radio, listening to television, watching movies, listening to announcements in public places, and so forth. To date it has been almost impossible to provide these sorts of experiences in the classroom. But with new video technology readily available, and relatively inexpensive in the new half-inch format, many of the sources of such input are indeed now usable in the classroom. The ideal would be to use video recordings of foreign language media, mainly television and movies, both of which include a wide variety of listening experiences, to teach listening skills that to now have been attainable only through extended residence in the target language culture.

In addition to the intrinsic value of listening skills, Krashen (1;2) has hypothesized that listening comprehension is the basis on which the acquisition process unfolds. His Input Hypothesis claims that the quality and quantity of output (speech) is crucially dependent on the quality and quantity of comprehensible input learners process. The prevailing view had been that the ability to speak depended exclusively on the opportunities provided to the students to speak. Without question, in order to develop speaking skills one must have opportunities to speak the target language; however, the Input Hypothesis claims that fluency is dependent on prior opportunities to process comprehensible input in the target language. If Krashen is correct, then increased listening skills should also result in increased fluency in speech.

The Students and the Course

The course was called "Spanish 15: Advanced Listening Skills." Although we used the number 15 to designate a "lower-division" course, the prerequisite was to have completed the equivalent of a second year of college Spanish. In fact, a majority of the thirteen students in the class were Spanish majors, most of whom had taken at least one upper-division course in literature, linguistics, or culture. All students who took the course had learned Spanish exclusively in the classroom: native speakers and students who had lived abroad in a Spanish-speaking country were excluded. In spite of the exclusions, the class was relatively heterogeneous with regard to overall language skills. The students' speaking skills ranged from intermediate-low to intermediate-high. The listening skills were slightly higher, from intermediate-mid to advanced, but only because the ACTFL Proficiency Guidelines for listening skills are, in this writer's opinion, too weak. (On this point, see Omaggio, 3.)

The course met twice per week for 2 hours each session. It met for either 100 minutes with no break or for 110 minutes with a 10-minute break, depending on what oral texts were being used. The 2-hour session was scheduled so that a complete feature-length movie could be shown during class. The class met for 10 weeks and the students received 4 quarter units of elective lower-division credit. Since this was an experimental class, units did not count toward the Spanish major.

The requirements for the course included attendance for the 40 hours of class instruction plus 60 hours of outside-of-class listening time. The 60 extra hours were in the form of video (taped from local Spanish-language television) and live television viewing for those students who had access to Spanish-language television at their place of residence. All video material was taped from live television broadcasts for later playback and then erased at the end of forty-five days in order to conform with copyright laws. This is inconvenient, to say the least, and at the present time we are working on putting together a collection of video materials without copyright problems. There are a number of good video programs available for purchase as well as subscription television materials broadcast by satellite. However, in order to keep the collection up to date, it will always be necessary to tape programs directly off the air. The wide availability of Spanish channels on cable in many cities makes this task much easier for Spanish teachers. Video equipment for the use of PAL/SECAM materials recorded in France or Germany is more expensive, but easily obtainable. A limited number of oral texts were used: (1) movies without subtitles, (2) an entire soap opera (*telenovela*) of about 60 hours, (3) news, (4) documentaries, (5) game shows, (6) variety shows, and (7) commercials.

There were four general types of class activities: (1) discussion of "key word" vocabulary from the oral text (video) to be viewed, (2) class viewing of oral texts, (3) oral followup summaries and discussion of the text viewed in class or as homework, usually in pairs first, then as a whole group, and (4) work on listening skills/techniques with the oral text. Types 2 and 3 are not controversial: the viewing of a text in class provides the opportunity for immediate interest in oral discussion in the target language. Types 1 and 4 require some additional justification.

When learners are faced with the task of comprehending an oral text, there are three factors that determine their ability to make sense of the input: (1) their choice of listening strategies, (2) their knowledge of the target language vocabulary and structure used in the input, and (3) the speed at which they are able to process the input utterances. The intermediate students, unlike beginners, needed little instruction in listening strategies, since most reported that even before taking the class they used key words and context to guess at global meaning. Their knowledge of Spanish structure was adequate, although it is impossible to know how often they used grammatical markers and structures in comprehension, since most grammar is redundant in communicative context.

What was clearly inadequate was their knowledge of common Spanish vocabulary. Words used in oral texts such as news broadcasts are not necessarily found in written texts frequently used in Spanish courses. Nor did the students recognize everyday household words such as *diapers, cabinet, scrub, trash,* so common in television commercials. In addition, words common to soap operas were mostly unknown to the students: *to deceive, to betray, to make jealous, inheritance, stepmother.* It is interesting that the number of this sort of words was relatively limited, and after the first twenty episodes or so with fifteen to twenty new key words per half-hour episode, the number of new words dropped dramatically to four or five new words per episode.

For most of the oral texts the instructor prepared a list of vocabulary words and expressions that were crucial to understanding the text. There was no attempt to include all new words in the oral text. Students reported that from one-fourth to one-half of the words in a given list were unfamiliar to them. The lists contained the Spanish word or expression, an English equivalent, and an illustrative sentence, usually taken directly from the oral text. Length ranged from about seventy-five words from a typical movie to two or three from a commercial. A news segment might yield three or four new words. Vocabulary discussion usually lasted from 10 to 15 minutes per class. Vocabulary quizzes were administered once every two weeks and consisted of words from the previous lists, which were to be defined and/or used in a sentence in a way that illustrated their meaning.

Although the single most important barrier to comprehension was lack of comprehension of individual key vocabulary items in the input, slow processing speed was clearly a problem. This problem is identifiable in the following way. Play a short oral text of 15 to 60 seconds, say a commercial, to the students. Stop the video at various points and ask the students to produce exactly what they have heard. The usual reaction the first time is that they didn't understand the part of the text you want them to repeat. Replay it for them and request an exact repetition. In some cases, they will now hear words they can repeat, but do not understand— this is the vocabulary problem mentioned above. In other cases, they will recognize all of the words in the utterance and after hearing it once or twice again, they will be able to do an exact repetition. This latter problem is one of process speed: they know the words and structures individually, but are not able to process them at normal broadcast speed.

The two problems are related; if they hear many words they do not recognize, they become confused and process speed slows down. If they are unable to process what they actually know fast enough, they are unable to use known language and context to guess at the meaning of items they do not know. If both vocabulary and process speed are weak, the input becomes a "blur" of target language with only a very few comprehensible parts, and frequently they are not able to process enough of the input to comprehend even the main points. The cure for slow process speed is simply practice and experience with more input. In the case of this group (intermediate–high, for the most part), most students reported dramatic increases in process speed after 30 to 50 hours of input, although most did not really begin to feel comfortable with the oral texts until the end of the quarter, after about 100 hours of input. From 100 to 200 hours of broadcast media input is necessary for intermediates to reach advanced levels of listening comprehension.

Results

In order to have an informal measure of the progress made by the students in Spanish 15, a listening exam was put together that consisted of four video texts and eighteen questions. The oral texts included parts from two different *telenovelas*, a movie, and a news broadcast. The questions required a written response. For example, the second question was *¿Cuánto durmió Jesús?* Answer: *casi nada.* The test took approximately 15 minutes to administer. It was administered to three groups twice: once at the beginning of the quarter and once at the end. The groups were the experimental group (the Spanish 15 class), the control nonnatives (all Spanish majors, but nonnatives), and the control native group (all Spanish majors, native speakers, most of whom were born and raised in the United States). The natives were chosen to give validity to the listening test itself as well as to measure the difference between hearing the material once and then repeated. There were 18 total points possible on the exams. The results of all tests are given in Figures 1 and 2.[1]

The mean increase between the pretest and posttest for both control groups was 4. This increase could have been due to a real increase in listening comprehension skills due to experiences during the quarter. However, since the native speakers also show an increase in the mean of 4, this increase is most likely due to the repetition of the same exam. The mean increase of the experimental group was exactly twice that of both control groups. Furthermore, the data show that the comprehension level of the experimental group at the beginning of the course was only slightly above that of the nonnative speaker control group, while at the end of the course it was almost the same as the native speaker group the first time they took the exam.[2]

Table 1
Raw Scores

Experimental (N = 10)			Control Nonnatives (N = 11)			Control Natives (N = 9)		
Name	Pre	Post	Name	Pre	Post	Name	Pre	Post
F	7	13	O	11	15.5	A	15	18
W	7	15	W	0	6.5	P	12	15
L	9	15	H	7	8	B	10	17
H	1	11.5	L	1	3.5	P	17	18
N	6	14.5	B	5	7	M	15	18
Y	7	18	W	3	9.5	M	17	17
Z	5	12	A	2	10	P	16	18
S	8	14	S	1	6.5	F	9	14
K	8	14	B	4	6.5	B	9	18
O	1	13	G	6	4			
			S	5	11			
Mean	6	14	Mean	4	8	Mean	13	17

Table 2
Comparison of Groups

	Pretest	Posttest	Mean Increase
Experimental	6	14	8
Control nonnatives	4	8	4
Control natives	13	17	4

The data indicate that listening comprehension training with video materials for intermediate students gives them experiences that cannot be duplicated in traditional classrooms limited to instructor–student interaction. In addition to increases in the ability to comprehend the target language as used in the media, students report three other gains: (1) a lowering of inhibitions to engage a native speaker in conversation, (2) a greater ability to understand native speakers in real conversations, and (3) an enhanced ability to speak. Although the data do not prove the last claim, such improvements were reported informally by most of the students and they are consistent with the predictions made by Krashen's Input Hypothesis.

Student Testimonials

Here are some excerpts from typical student comments:

GW: When watching TV I could understand what was happening from observing the situation, but my comprehension of the spoken word was probably only about 40 percent. Now I would say that my comprehension is about 75 to 100 percent. Since taking this course, I feel much more at ease with native speakers.

CN: When I began this class I could understand very, very little of what I watched on TV....I couldn't understand a *telenovela* really at all. I couldn't separate the words in a newscast. Now I can follow dialogs and pick out separate words that I don't understand rather than hearing whole sentences without separating the words and understanding nothing. I can listen to the news and understand a lot of it easily. Most commercials I can understand completely.

LH: I usually was able to understand the main idea of something, but the details were vague. Now things are so much easier that I find myself tuning unimportant parts out. Before I couldn't find the unimportant parts.

BL: I could understand really well in classroom situations but in conversations with people (with me listening rather than as an active participant) I was usually only able to understand about half of what was happening. Now...I feel that I can understand Spanish a lot better. I feel that I might even be getting over my fear of speaking.

RO: When I entered this class I understood...what was said after several times through. Sometimes I didn't even understand what you (the instructor) were saying. Now I can usually understand what is going on and get the gist of what they are saying and often understand all or most of it.

JS: At the beginning of class I could understand more of the type of Spanish that one would typically hear in a class at school. Now I find that I can understand a lot more not only of spoken Spanish but written Spanish as well. The same is true when I sit down to write something in Spanish. My spoken Spanish has improved and I can understand Spanish speakers better. I still don't understand everything, but I do understand much more. I can understand most of the ideas....I can now, and probably will, watch Spanish TV and understand it.

LF: I feel my comprehension of Spanish has increased a lot. I've especially noticed that it takes much less effort for me to understand.

YL: When I began this class, I couldn't understand the [video] tapes...where a higher level...of vocabulary was used. Now my understanding runs from fairly good to almost understanding all that is said. Also I have learned to pay really good attention to what is being said.

MG: I comprehend Spanish very well now. I feel more confident when I turn on Spanish TV. It seems when I was watching the commercials lately, I understood almost everything.

LK: When I spoke with my Mexican or Argentinean friends I always understood them because they spoke to me so that I would. But when they spoke to one another, it always seemed like some other new foreign language. I can see my comprehension has increased immensely. I also noticed an improvement in my reading comprehension, which is very nice. I can understand the whole idea of the sections...before I would concentrate on certain words and worry about understanding them, but now I listen to the whole idea.

LZ: After taking this course I understand what is being said on the Spanish programs with much less difficulty....It is enjoyable for me to watch the Spanish programs now. It is also easier for me to understand my professor in one class.

Although video courses such as the one described here require a large amount of advanced preparation time, they are, for students without experience living in the target language culture, the only way to move students from an intermediate level to an advanced level in listening skills.

Notes

1. Only 10 of the 13 students enrolled took both the pre- and posttests.
2. Tests were not run on the data because of the low number of students involved in the experiment. However, from the limited data available and the comments by the students themselves, it is clear that the improvement in listening skills was dramatic.

References

1. Krashen, Stephen. *Principles and Practice in Second Language Acquisition.* Oxford: Pergamon, 1982.
2. _____. *The Input Hypothesis: Issues and Implications.* London: Longman, 1987.
3. Omaggio, Alice C. *Teaching Language in Context: Proficiency-Oriented Instruction.* Boston: Heinle and Heinle, 1986.

3
Developing Extensive Reading Skills: The Transition to Literature

Julie A. Storme
St. Mary's College, Notre Dame, Indiana
H. Jay Siskin
Northwestern University, Evanston, Illinois

For many years after the audiolingual revolution, reading was considered to be a passive skill, a process that was supposed to "take care of itself." If students learned to speak, they would be able to read. Recent research has reformulated entirely our understanding of the reading skill and has given us new insights into the strategies that effective readers use. Reading is not a passive skill, but rather an interactive process between reader and text (Barnitz, 5; Coady, 9; Phillips, 17; Smith, 21).

Goodman's (10) psycholinguistic reading model represents the reading process as one of sampling, predicting, testing, and confirming. The fluent reader does not process a text by identifying and interpreting each and every letter and word sequence. This word-by-word decoding is a poor strategy that overemphasizes the linguistic component of reading and leads to poor comprehension. Indeed, according to Swaffar, familiarity with "the words" will not prevent misconstrued meanings (23, p. 126). Effective readers free themselves from decoding by taking a sample of the text and predicting the meaning and direction of a larger part of it. Once a prediction has taken place, its accuracy must be tested, based on previous information in the text or knowledge of the world. If the prediction is confirmed, the sampling cycle begins again. If there is some inaccuracy or inconsistency, the reader may choose to reread the passage, to suspend belief, or to revise expectations (see Goodman, 10). Thus, proficient readers comprehend by actively constructing and revising models of meaning as they read. In the words of Smith, a reader "brings meaning to print" (21, p. 2. See also Adams and Collins, 1). Although proficient readers will guess incorrectly or have moments of uncertainty, they will recover quickly. Poor readers, on the other hand, will be lost in a cycle of wrong previous information leading to a successive series of wrong predictions (Coady, 9).

What factors enter into the development of the proficient reader? Study after study points to the essential role of background knowledge, indicating that we can only comprehend when we can relate a text to something we already know. (See, for example, Ausubel, 3 and 4; Carrell, 6 and 7; Coady, 9; Johnson, 12; Levine and Haus, 13; Steffensen and Joag-Dev, 22.) Background knowledge may include linguistic knowledge, such as lexical meaning, word derivation, syntactic rules, and verb tenses; but its scope is necessarily much larger, including readers' "general experience of the world," as Phillips notes (17, p. 285). This general experience is organized into schemata or mental constructs of meaning (see Nelson, 15, among many others). Interaction between schemata and text guides a reader's interpretation, resulting in effective comprehension (see Adams and Collins, 1; Carrell, 7; and Swaffar, 23).

In addition to this process of schematizing, the proficient reader relies upon other strategies, such as discourse organization and synthesizing, as well as skimming, scanning, and gisting skills. (See Carrell, 7; Grellet, 11.) Proficient readers, then, have a repertoire of tools at their disposal, but this is not the case for students learning to read in a foreign language. Clarke points out that "limited control over the language 'short-circuits' the good reader's system, causing the reader to revert to poor reading strategies when confronted with a difficult or confusing task in the second language" (8, p. 206). Our task as teachers is to assist students in their effort to acquire the skills and strategies necessary to effective reading. Clearly, in Phillips's words, "we can no longer assume that reading 'will just happen'" (17, p. 295).

In fact, there has been a strong response to the recent research on the reading skill that has led to the development of many exciting new methods and materials. Thanks to authors such as Grellet (11), Omaggio (16), Phillips (17), and others, instructors now have available to them a variety of suggestions to improve intensive reading skills. These approaches, however, have for the most part concentrated on short authentic texts and intensive reading strategies—leaving a serious gap in extensive reading and encouraging a shift away from literary texts. This is particularly apparent in the newest readers; the vast majority include no literary selections at all, or they include only short extracts. Decrying the days when we struggled through a Molière play or some other complete literary text with our intermediate language classes, some argue that the teaching of the reading skill need not—even should not—include literary texts.

Although literary studies have been overemphasized in the past, their complete elimination is unjustifiably extreme. The fact is that in most university foreign language departments the bulk of the course offerings are literary. These are required courses for literature majors; language/ culture options normally have a literature component as well. Further- more, to ignore literature is to deprive students of culturally significant and authentic texts. Finally, literary texts foster the development of extensive reading skills, which are necessary to both reading for professional purposes and reading for pleasure. Furthermore, let us not forget that there are actually students who enjoy reading literature!

Reading literature requires well-developed extensive reading skills; if we are to continue teaching literary texts, we must teach students how to read them. Unfortunately, despite all the energy that has been directed at reformulating our approach to reading, students going beyond basic language courses still lack training in extensive reading. Schulz describes how our neglect places an unfair burden on the students who continue their study:

> [The students] are usually started without mercy on the chronological study of the literary masterworks of the target language in a survey course. Suddenly, instructors expect a transition from the stage of painful word-by-word decoding of contrived written dialogs or narrations dealing with simple everyday events to comprehension of relatively lengthy literary texts contain- ing highly abstract vocabulary, complex syntactical patterns, and sophisticated style and content which even an educated native speaker often cannot read without effort (19, p. 43).

The gap in teacher expectations and student preparedness sets up a cycle of frustration that Schulz identifies as an important factor in the attrition rate of upper-level courses. Even with the very best training in intensive reading, students would still feel the frustration described by Schulz once they began to study longer texts. We can no longer continue asking students to learn literary traditions while their reading skills are only partially in place. Clearly, we must provide a transition from intensive to extensive reading.

An effective method for teaching extensive reading must explicitly establish the goals of skill development and process strategies, thereby delaying the traditional "discussion of the text" until the students have had a chance to acquire the necessary reading skills. In such an approach, the teacher's role is reformulated: We must first establish students' awareness and understanding of the role of process strategies as well as illustrate effective strategies (Loew, 14); also, we must provide opportunities for students to develop their own strategies.

Awareness and sensitivity to the role of process strategies is of the utmost importance since, as Swaffar points out, students cannot schematize unless they intend to do so (23, p. 126). Phillips likens the teachers' efforts to "pump-priming" in order to "bring to the surface the special knowledge banks needed by learners" (17, pp. 286–87). This "pump-priming" begins with the teacher's example and continues with exercises that foster skill development. Finally, as Phillips recommends, these reading comprehension exercises must "project the learner through several phases of the reading process" (17, p. 293).

The method we propose[1] addresses these requirements by establishing a five-stage cycle in which each stage concentrates on a particular set of strategies, thereby emphasizing their primacy to the students. The successive stages activate student background knowledge at every level. The first three stages consist of prereading exercises, a stage overwhelmingly recommended in the current body of research (Grellet, 11; Omaggio, 16; Phillips, 17; and many others). The cyclical nature of the approach stresses the interdependency of extensive reading skills, giving students the capacity to interpret "multiple cues" and providing "a global approach," both of which are seen by Loew (14), Phillips (17), Schulz (20), and others as necessary elements. We preface the description of our approach by considering the selection of the text.

Selecting the Text

In order to read literary texts[2] effectively, students require experimentation in guided trial and error with a variety of texts (Swaffar, 23). It is particularly important that more than one text be used so that the learning task is not focused on the comprehension of *one particular text.* The goal of an extensive reading course must be larger in scope, concentrating on strategies applicable to any literary text. Given the fact that students are going to read very slowly at this point, and therefore time constraints make it impractical to read three or four literary texts in their entirety over the course of a single semester, we suggest that each text be taught through a series of extracts taken from three to five literary texts.

It is essential that the extracts from any single text convey a sense of continuity, forming as much as possible an abridged version of the entire text. Each extract, then, must not be self-contained, but should build upon the previous extract(s), requiring the students to treat them as a single text rather than as four or five separate texts. This selection process is not an easy one and must be carefully considered; much will necessarily be sacrificed in our "abridged" version of the text. What will determine the choice is the concept of *script.*

We define script as predictable, stereotypic sequences of events or patterns of behavior appropriate to a particular historical or social context. Knowledge of a script shapes our expectations and defines parameters: we are able to replace details omitted from the story, supply connections, and evaluate the events that take place (Schank, 18, pp. 101–2; Swaffar, 23, p. 125). It enables us to read more proficiently, since we can make more accurate predictions about the direction of the text (Swaffar, 23, p. 126).

A novel such as *Les Liaisons dangereuses* offers any number of scripts from which you may choose: seduction, betrayal, initiation, manipulation, etc. Your script selection serves as a guideline to determine which episodes in the novel will form your series of extracts. Thus, if you choose the seduction script, you could include the following scenes: the marquise's seduction of Cécile, the marquise's seduction of Prévan, Valmont's seduction of Cécile, or Valmont's seduction of Mme de Tourvel.

SCRIPT: *Seduction of a Virtuous Woman*

Extract 1: Valmont forms his plan
         Letters IV, VI, XXI, XXII, XXIII

Extract   2: Valmont's   confession   of   love   and   the   initial
         correspondence
         Letters XXIV, XXVI, XXXIII–XXXVI

Extract 3: La Présidente asks Valmont to leave and the correspondence continues
Letters XXXVII, XL–XLIII
Valmont reads La Présidente's letters
Letter XLIV

Extract 4: After a few weeks' absence, Valmont decides to return and continues to pursue La Présidente
Letters LXXVI–LXXVIII, XC, XCIX

Extract 5: La Présidente flees, confessing her love for Valmont to Mme de Rosemonde
Letters C, CII

Extract 6: The seduction
Letter CXXV

Extract 7: Valmont betrays la Présidente
Letters CXXXV, CXXXVII–CXXXVIII
The final "rupture"
Letters CXLI–CXLIII
La Présidente's death
Letters CXLVII, CLXV

Although chronology will normally determine the sequence of the extracts, it need not necessarily be strictly adhered to in this case: it might prove more useful to teach Valmont's seductions of Mme de Tourvel in an uninterrupted sequence or to place any episodes that significantly expand the notion of the script, such as the marquise's seduction of Cécile, toward the end of the sequence. Chronology is more restrictive if you attempt to convey a more complete notion of plot through the series of extracts. Thus, if you choose the script of betrayal for *La Chanson de Roland,* you would choose episodes that trace the development of Ganelon's betrayal; whereas the same script for *Les Liaisons dangereuses* would probably call for scenes of various betrayals occurring throughout the novel.

SCRIPT: Betrayal and Revenge

Extract 1: The plot, strophes 1–7 and 9–10
The choice of Ganelon, strophes 12–46
The betrayal, strophes 52 and 54

Extract 2: The choice of Roland and his departure, strophes 58–69
The Sarrasins prepare for battle, strophes 76 and 79
The battle, strophes 81–84, 88, 89, 93, 104, 105, 107, 111, and 112
Roland sounds his horn, strophes 128–143

Extract 3: The death of Oliver, strophes 145, 146, 148–150
Roland in battle, strophes 156–157

Extract 4: The death of Turpin, strophes 161–164, 166, and 168
The death of Roland, strophes 173–176 and 177
Charlemagne pursues the Sarrasins, strophes 179–181

Extract 5: The return to Ronceveaux, strophes 203–205, 213–214
The battle with the Sarrasins, strophes 216, 225–226, 228, 261–265
The return to France and the judgment of Ganelon, strophes 270–280, 285–287

Thus, the connection among the extracts may be thematic or based on plot, but each extract must require the students to recall information from previous extracts. This is of primary importance, since a skill particular to extensive reading is the ability to recall and synthesize information or ideas presented in earlier portions of the text.

Stage One: Predicting

The first set of prereading exercises, always done in class *before* students have read the text, is a prediction exercise. The goals of this exercise are to develop the skill of schematizing and to familiarize students with the script by calling upon their preexisting knowledge of the world. In some instances, the title serves as an excellent script activator; a good deal of discussion, for instance, can be generated by the title *Le Bourgeois gentilhomme*.

The discussion begins with the meaning of *bourgeois* and then progresses to its social implications. The instructor might ask the class what differences there are between the implications of *bourgeois* for American culture and those for French culture, or between modern France and seventeenth century France. The discussion then proceeds to the word *gentilhomme*: the instructor asks several questions about the connotations of this part of the title: What characteristics do you expect a gentleman to have or what kind of social status do you associate with the word *gentilhomme*? The next step is to lead students into a discussion of the implications of combining these words in a single title.

SCRIPT: Portrait of an Arriviste

Extract 1: The "maîtres" ridicule M. Jourdain, Act One, Scene I
M. Jourdain is instructed by his "maîtres," Act Two, Scenes I–IV

Extract 2: Dorante borrows money from M. Jourdain; portrait of Dorante, Act Three, Scene IV
M. Jourdain and Dorante discuss the arrival of the marquise, Scene VI

Extract 3: Mme Jourdain and Nicole: their suspicions of M. Jourdain; discussions of the marriages between Lucile and Cléonte/Nicole and Covielle, Act Three, Scene VII
Cléonte asks for Lucile's hand; M. Jourdain refuses, Scenes XI–XII

Extract 4: Covielle disguised as a Turk: the son of the Grand Turk asks to marry Lucile, Act Four, Scene V
The three marriages arranged; resolution, Act Five, Scenes VI–VII

Prediction Exercises
Title:

1. What does the word *bourgeois* mean to you?
2. List three adjectives that might describe a "gentleman" for you.
3. In what ways might a gentleman be *bourgeois*?
4. In English, the title of this work is *The Would-Be Gentleman*. What does this mean to you? In what sense could this title be the equivalent of *Le Bourgeois gentilhomme*?

5. If someone is striving to be a gentleman, what attitude might be assumed toward those around him?

Act One, Scene I:

6. What attitude might cultured people take toward a wealthy man who is trying to acquire culture?

Act Three, Scene IV:

7. Why might people try to curry favor with M. Jourdain? What social advantage does he possess?

8. How might they go about obtaining favor with him? How would he respond?

Scene VII:

9. Given M. Jourdain's social pretensions, what type of husband would he seek for his daughter?

Act Four, Scene V:

10. By what means could M. Jourdain be manipulated? Which of his weaknesses could be exploited?

In other instances, the instructor will need to provide the students with background knowledge they do not possess before an effective discussion can be launched. It is appropriate, for instance, to describe the genre of the *chanson de geste* and to inform students of oral traditions of literature in the Middle Ages before considering the title La Chanson de Roland.

The range of aspects of the script to be covered is broad, including conventions pertinent to events, situations, behavior, characters, etc., and must be determined by the instructor according to the needs of the particular text. It would be appropriate before reading the first extract of *La Chanson de Roland* to initiate a discussion concerning characters. The instructor informs the students that the protagonists of the text are for the most part *chevaliers* or knights and then asks them what characteristics, settings, or themes they associate with knights. The instructor's role alternates between providing partial information to students and responding to student input. Students will require considerable correction, since their knowledge of knights may not fully correspond to the *chevaliers* of *La Chanson de Roland*.

Prediction Exercises for La Chanson de Roland

Extract 1:.   What characteristics (characters, settings, themes, rhetorical devices) do you expect to find in this text given the fact that it is a *chanson de geste*? How do the section titles (e.g., the betrayal) help you predict what will happen?

Extract 2.   In this extract, Ganelon returns to Charlemagne's camps. Given what takes place in the first extract, what do you expect Ganelon to do? When do you next expect to see the Sarrasins and King Marsile? Also, there is an important battle scene in this extract. How do you expect the characters to behave in battle? What do you expect to happen in this battle?

Extracts 3 and 4.   In these extracts, Turpin, Oliver and Roland die. Make predictions regarding their deaths. How do you expect them to die, of what cause(s), and how do you expect them to behave at death?

Extract 5.   How do you expect the *chanson* to end?

We must also keep in mind that scripts change over time: the script for "a battle" has changed significantly from the Middle Ages to the present time. Finally, while students may be familiar with events or behavior, they may not be acquainted with their literary encoding, which likewise may call up a series of stereotypic behaviors. This should not be seen as a failure on either the students' or instructor's part, but rather as an essential step enabling the students to comprehend the text more fully.

With the first extract, these prediction exercises amount to guided brainstorming based on title, genre, character, literary period, or any other organizing device that would prove effective for the text in question. The prediction exercises for subsequent extracts should always be based at least partially on knowledge gained from the prior extract(s). By asking students to predict events that would flow logically from prior episodes, students develop the ability to identify textual shape and logic, encouraging them to see relations among separate sections of the text.[3] For instance, the instructor would inform the class that the next extract of *La Chanson de Roland* they are going to read is a battle scene and then ask students to predict how the *chevaliers* will behave in battle given their portrait in the first extract. Once again, the instructor's role is to provide initial information to launch the discussion and to subsequently guide the discussion in a fruitful direction by responding critically to student input.

These successive prediction exercises will necessarily "give away the ending" to some extent. This is not a problem, since prior knowledge of the text does not undermine the reading process; rather anticipation and formation of textual expectations improves comprehension (see Phillips, 17, p. 289).

These prereading exercises and later postreading exercises should be performed in the native tongue, since discussion in the foreign language renders total concentration on reading skills virtually impossible. As Phillips argues, "In the second language classroom, the reading skills need to be developed in an isolated—that is concentrated—fashion. Tasks that are only peripheral to reading comprehension easily sidetrack the learner" (17, p. 286; see also Swaffar, 23, pp. 125 and 138).

Stage Two: Intensive Reading Strategies

Intensive reading cannot be abandoned altogether in this methodology, despite its emphasis on extensive reading, since attention to detail is crucial in order to confirm or reject constructs of meaning. Exercises that develop intensive reading skills have been outlined in numerous works (Grellet, 11; Omaggio, 16; Phillips, 17) and may include exercises requiring students to guess meaning from context, to derive meaning on the basis of sentence structure, to recognize rhetorical patterns or discourse organization, or to answer detailed comprehension questions. These reading exercises, however, should not be the first set of exercises performed for an extract, since this would wrongly shift the emphasis to intensive reading; rather they are prereading exercises to be offered sometime after the prediction exercises.

Intensive Reading Exercises for La Chanson de Roland

I. Determine the meaning of the following words from the surrounding context: *otages, un destrier, chevaucher, messe et matines.*

II. Textual Cues

1. "La nuit s'achève, et l'aube claire apparaît." Use the structure of the sentence in combination with familiar vocabulary to determine the meaning of this sentence.

2. "...ni palefroi ni destrier ni mule ni mulet roussin ni cheval de somme." Find the common element in this list to help you understand unfamiliar vocabulary.

3. During the battle the French cry out, "Honni soit qui fuira!" What might this mean?

4. "Eh! Durendal, comme tu es belle et sainte! En ton pommeau d'or il y a quantité de reliques, une dent de saint Pierre, du sang de saint Basile, des cheveux de monseigneur saint Denis, de vêtement de Sainte Marie."
   What is the common element of this list? "Who" is Durendal and what does Durendal have to do with this list?

Stage Three: Extensive Reading Strategies

The goal of these exercises is to help students develop speed and to teach them to focus on global comprehension without being impeded by detail. Appropriate exercises include (1) gisting, an exercise that emphasizes global comprehension; students are asked to read for general information and to provide a summary of the passage; (2) skimming, an activity that asks students to read with somewhat more focus, providing information such as listing the main ideas or identifying the characters and setting; (3) scanning, in which students search for specific points such as an important transition, an introduction of a theme, or a crucial detail. The time allotted for these exercises should be limited, since they are designed in part to help students develop reading speed. In addition, these exercises teach students that comprehension and meaning do not depend on grasping every detail. (See Schulz, 20, p. 128.) Thus, students learn to shift their focus beyond the level of the word.

Extensive Reading Exercises for La Chanson de Roland

1. Read the first two sentences of strophe 9. On the basis of these sentences, what can you conclude with regard to the previous actions, the present setting, and the present action?

2. Read the first and last two sentences of strophe 79. What can you conclude about the content of this strophe? Rapidly scan the strophe to find the transition sentence.

3. Rapidly read strophe 111. What is the gist? What is the strophe's focus?

4. In strophe 177, Charlemagne returns to Ronceveaux. What do you expect him to do? Verify your predictions by rapidly reading strophe 179.

5. What is the importance of strophe 228? Why is it included in the *chanson?*

Stage Four: Verification

The initial prediction exercises will be followed by a reading assignment, the extract, which will be followed in turn by a postreading exercise in which students are asked to verify and/or modify the predictions made prior to the reading. The goal of this set of exercises is twofold: to allow students to articulate what and how they understood; and subsequently to have students analyze their previous predictions and their textual comprehension. They need to identify their errors and why they made them. Thus, articulation requires students to focus on process and gives the teacher insight into their routes to meaning (Phillips, 17, p. 285).[4]

Since students are asked to guess about the text before they've read it and since the postreading verification/modification exercises depend in part upon errors having been made, they are particularly useful to the very careful learner who is traditionally more comfortable with controlled grammatical exercises and is often unable to take the risks that are an essential part of effective reading. These students' discomfort with risk taking can be reduced by this type of exercise where a "wrong" answer can be just as productive as a "right" answer. (See Phillips, 17; Schulz, 20; and Swaffar, 23.)

Stage Five: Transition to Literature

We end our cycle where the literature classes traditionally begin, with a set of comprehension and discussion questions. These exercises have three purposes: to teach students to make connections between parts of a text, to make the transition from comprehension to textual analysis, and to familiarize students with literary metalanguage. Furthermore, these exercises require the students to reread the series of extracts using the reading strategies that have been developed over the course of the cycle. At this point, students have a well-developed knowledge of the text's script and are able to synthesize diverse elements of the text into a coherent construct of meaning.

Transition-to-Literature Exercises for La Chanson de Roland

1. How are the Sarrasins portrayed? In what ways are the readers' opinions of the Sarrasins influenced?
2. How is Charlemagne portrayed?
3. Look for rhetorical devices typical of the epic genre (repetition, exaggeration, epithets, etc.).
4. How does medieval warfare differ from our modern notions of warfare? What's the archbishop's role in the battle?
5. How do you understand Roland's refusal to blow his horn? How can you explain his later decision to sound the horn; what makes him change his mind?
6. What's the significance of the description of Roland's death?

Steps for Teaching Extensive Reading

(Select extracts based on concept of script)

Prereading exercises:
1. Prediction exercises
2. Intensive reading exercises
3. Extensive reading exercises

Postreading activities:
4. Verification/modification
5. Transition to literature

(Repeat procedure for subsequent extracts)

Conclusion

In the past students who have learned to read literary texts have been self-taught for the most part, acquiring effective strategies through unguided trial and error. This is usually a long, difficult, and discouraging process. We need to teach the joy rather than the pain of reading so that we can encourage rather than discourage interested students. By activating students' knowledge of script and process strategies, we make a productive step in this direction.

Notes

1. This method has been classroom tested at St. Mary's College over a three-year period following the equivalent of two years of college study.
2. The definition of literary texts is broad and may include philosophical and historical texts as well as those most often labeled "literary," the principal requirements being that the texts are of sufficient length that they call for extensive reading skills and that they not be read solely for the extraction of specific information.
3. Swaffar asserts that the ability to identify textual logic enhances recall (23, p. 129).
4. Aspatore (2) rightly identifies this as an important step toward shifting the emphasis from right and wrong answers to the process of reading.

References

1. Adams, Marilyn, and Allan Collins. "A Schema-Theoretic View of Reading," pp. 1–21 in Roy O. Freedle, ed., *New Directions in Discourse Processing*. Norwood, NJ: Ablex, 1979.
2. Aspatore, Jilleen V. "But I Don't Know All the Words." *Foreign Language Annals* 17 (1984):297–99.
3. Ausubel, David. "The Use of Advance Organizers in the Learning and Retention of Meaningful Verbal Material." *Journal of Educational Psychology* 51 (1960):267–72.
4. _____. *Educational Psychology: A Cognitive View*. New York: Holt, Rinehart and Winston, 1968.
5. Barnitz, John G. "Toward Understanding the Effects of Cross-Cultural Schemata and Discourse Structure on Second-Language Reading Comprehension." *Journal of Reading Behavior* 18 (1986):95–116.
6. Carrell, Patricia. "Three Components of Background Knowledge in Reading Comprehension." *Language Learning* 33 (1983):183–207.
7. _____. "Schema Theory and ESL Reading: Classroom Implications and Applications." *Modern Language Journal* 68 (1984):332–43.
8. Clarke, Mark A. "The Short-Circuit Hypothesis of ESL Reading—Or When Language Competence Interferes with Reading Performance." *Modern Language Journal* 64 (1980):203–9.
9. Coady, James. "A Psycholinguistic Model of the ESL Reader," pp. 5–18 in MacKay, Barkman, and Jordan, eds., *Reading in a Second Language*. Rowley, MA: Newbury House, 1979.
10. Goodman, Kenneth S. "The Psycholinguistic Nature of the Reading Process," pp. 15–26 in Goodman, ed., *The Psycholinguistic Nature of the Reading Process*. Detroit: Wayne State University Press, 1968.
11. Grellet, Françoise. *Developing Reading Skills: A Practical Guide to Reading Comprehension Exercises*. Cambridge: Cambridge University Press, 1981.
12. Johnson, Patricia. "Effects on Reading Comprehension of Building Background Knowledge." *TESOL Quarterly* 16 (1982):503–16.
13. Levine, Martin, and George Haus. "The Effect of Background Knowledge on the Reading Comprehension of Second Language Learners." *Foreign Language Annals* 18 (1985):391–97.

14. Loew, Helene Z. "Developing Strategic Reading Skills." *Foreign Language Annals* 17 (1984): 301–3.

15. Nelson, Gayle L. "Culture's Role in Reading Comprehension: A Schema Theoretical Approach." *Journal of Reading* 30 (1987):424–29.

16. Omaggio, Alice. *Teaching Language in Context*. Boston: Heinle and Heinle, 1986.

17. Phillips, June K. "Practical Implications of Recent Research in Reading." *Foreign Language Annals* 17 (1984):285–96.

18. Schank, Roger. *Reading and Understanding*. Hillsdale, NJ: Lawrence Erlbaum, 1982.

19. Schulz, Renate A. "Literature and Readability: Bridging the Gap in Foreign Language Reading." *Modern Language Journal* 65 (1981):43–53.

20. _____. "Language Reading Instruction after the Elementary Course." *Modern Language Journal* 67 (1983):127–34.

21. Smith, Frank. *Understanding Reading*. New York: Holt, Rinehart and Winston, 1978.

22. Steffensen, Margaret S., and Chitra Joag-Dev. "Cultural Knowledge and Reading," pp. 48–61 in J. Charles Alderson and A. H. Urquhart, eds., *Reading in a Foreign Language*. New York: Longman, 1984.

23. Swaffar, Janet K. "Readers, Texts and Second Languages: The Interactive Processes." *Modern Language Journal* 72 (1988):123–49.

4
Global Education in the Language Classroom: The African Connection[1]

Millie Park Mellgren
University of Minnesota, Minneapolis

"Africa? But I'm a Spanish teacher!"

Nearly every student going through a second language teacher-education program proclaims that one of the main reasons that students *need* to study a second language is to promote world understanding through learning about other people and cultures of the world. Most practicing language teachers would agree that this is indeed an important aspect of language study. However, many of us go through our careers teaching about the "target" culture as a separate entity from the rest of the world. The usual comparison with American culture is made, but "culture" lessons are rarely integrated with the idea of the world as an interdependent society.

The word "culture" today has a different definition than it did in the past. Anderson (2, p. 15) states that humans live their lives in a "cocoon of culture whose circumference equals the circumference of the globe." In other words, a global culture. Countries do not exist in a vacuum without contact with the rest of the world, but rather all countries, no matter how remote, exist in an interdependent world. Remy (14) proposes that teachers approach lessons with a "world as systems" approach rather than the more traditional "world as nations" approach. The process of developing awareness in students of the interdependent global society should focus on coping with current major problems and alternatives leading to cooperation in the world (Brodbelt, 4). As teachers, we have the responsibility to be informed ourselves on global issues so that we can inform students when possible and help them find ways to make a difference in the direction the world is headed (Marker, 13).

As language teachers, we often feel that students indeed need to learn about the global society, but we find that the curriculum is already too crowded and that students will probably learn these important lessons "somewhere else," mainly social studies classes. Lamy (12) has proclaimed that global education is interdisciplinary and not limited to social studies if it is done properly. An important part of the globalization of the language-study curriculum would involve not only a study of the target culture but, as Fonte (9, p. 109) proclaims, would "give students the world picture as seen through the eyes of other peoples." In other words, how do the French look at what is happening on the world scene? How do Mexicans view the situation in the Middle East? Do the events in Central America have any impact on German society? Questions like these emphasize the nature of world interdependence and promote thought about the "target" culture as a part of the global society. Global education *is* part of the responsibility of language teachers and should not be crowded out of the curriculum due to lack of time or energy.

How does one include global education in the language classroom and what features should be included? First, as with any aspect of curriculum planning, one must state goals and purposes and recognize the magnitude of world views included in this area (Lamy, 12). Kobus (11), in a review of the literature, states that evaluations of existing programs and curricula suggest that an analysis of cultural differences within the context of universal characteristics is successful.

Global education, along with international relations, has been taught as an "observer sport" according to Alger (1, p. 58). People believe that "experts" in distant cities are concerned with the issues, and even though these same people may believe that issues affect them, they often do not see the link between their daily lives and these worldwide power centers. Global education must be concerned with teaching about the "links," not only among cultures but among the "powers" and the average citizen. Collins lists the following as important features of global education (7, p. 16–17):

1. Pay special attention to the concepts of "systems" and "interdependence" and emphasize that problems, choices, and solutions are interconnected and must be dealt with in an integrated manner.
2. Be future oriented and include consideration of the unintended or unanticipated outcomes ("surprise" effects) of our present actions.
3. View *all* subject areas as sources of data and not be limited to traditional content or sources of information.
4. Focus on a limited number of major concepts that are repeated at multiple grade levels.
5. Include the study of important global issues at levels of sophistication suitable to the age and interests of students.
6. Concern itself with informal, out-of-school learning and use the local community as a minilab.
7. Feature cross-cultural awareness and consideration of other people's perceptions of issues and realities in a multiethnic, pluralistic society and world.
8. Teach that individual humans—men and women equally—can make a difference, while avoiding unwarranted optimism or excessive pessimism.
9. Build on a solid knowledge and understanding of the local community, the state, and the nation as prerequisites to global understanding.

More simply stated by Becker and Anderson (3, p. 90):

1. Individuals need to begin in childhood and to expand in adolescence an understanding of the fact that the world is a singular, complex system.
2. Individuals need to begin in childhood and to expand in adolescence an understanding of the fact that they are participants in the global system.

To many teachers these goals may seem necessary and important but somewhat unrealistic to attempt in the classroom. One question often asked is "How can I possibly keep up on all the events in the world and be knowledgeable on global issues?" This indeed would be a monumental task for teachers who are spending plenty of valuable time already creating important materials and activities in their language classes. Fortunately, the nature of global education does *not* require the teacher to have all the information, but encourages students to explore, ask questions, and investigate the issues on their own. The teacher merely needs to spark the interest!

Seelye (15) presents two approaches for including global education in the second language curriculum. First, teachers can attempt to complete existing course objectives by including examples, visuals, activities, and ideas that cause students to think about other areas of the world. Second, teachers can develop new course objectives that allow global units to fit into the current curriculum. Either approach would help teachers make time for including world issues in their courses. In addition, if teachers would look at many of their present communicative activities and cultural lessons with "global eyes," they may find that there are many places where a slight twist of the content may change the activity to incorporate a global lesson as well.

The challenge is to get started and begin implementing the globalization of our language classes. We cannot just sit back and wait for someone else to teach our students about the world. We must take responsibility for the important contribution that we, as language teachers, can make to this important aspect of our students' education. As Cogan (6, p. 11) states, "Above all, don't be overwhelmed. Begin slowly, do a little at a time, and gradually the big picture will develop."

The African Example

Africa, though a massive continent, is an area of the world that many of our students know little about other than recognition of exotic animals or famine victims in Ethiopia. In a recent survey of second language teacher-education candidates it was found that while 68 percent of the students could name at least five African countries, only 52 percent could answer specific questions related to important people or locations in Africa. While these are not disastrous results, it is disheartening when one considers that foreign language teachers are viewed as being at least slightly more globally aware than the average population. Africa, therefore, becomes an ideal place to begin in the globalization of the classroom, because teachers can learn along with their students and increase their own global awareness.

Initially, it is a good idea to sit down and brainstorm all the connections you can think of between the target culture and Africa. This is difficult, but it offers a reasonable place to start. Often, when faced with this task, teachers think of few connections at first but find that the list grows if they keep with it. As with all brainstorming, this activity works best if it can be completed with colleagues, friends, students, or any others who can provide ideas to add to your list. French teachers must be careful not to focus only on French-speaking countries but note that they already have "a foot in the door" in creating connections between other African countries and French-speaking cultures.

Your list of African connections may include:

French:
- French defense agreements with a large number of African countries
- France as one of the largest exporters of weapons to African nations
- Maintained interest in former French colonies
- Canadian corp of volunteers in Africa
- Heavy French reliance on African minerals
- French construction of nuclear power plants in South Africa

German:
- Large volume of German tourism in Kenya
- Large German corp of volunteers in Africa
- Maintained interest in former German colonies
- Numerous speakers of German in Africa
- Large volume of trade and investment with South Africa
- Heavy involvement in transfer of technology and expertise to South Africa

Spanish:
- The Cuban involvement in Angola, Ethiopia, Mozambique, and other countries
- Long trade history between Spain and African countries
- Strong Nigerian ties with Latin America
- Argentinean weapons exports to South Africa
- Enormous soccer interest in Africa
- Security interests in South Atlantic between South Africa, Brazil, and Argentina

This is only an example of the numerous connections that can be made between Africa and other cultures. The list of connections you create can form the basis for creating new activities, for providing topics for oral or written communication and dialog, or for including new global content in existing course activities.

Another means for beginning to implement activities of a global nature is to think of a variety of *topics* that would lead to discussions, reading, writing, and other language-skill activities among students. Topics might include social class, population growth, hunger, foreign debt, militarization, religion, and gender roles, among other issues. With these topics in mind, it may be useful to create activities that utilize students' language skills to investigate and discuss the issues. It is important, however, not to *wait* to try global activities until students' language skills are highly developed. As Seelye (15) maintains, we must begin teaching culture as soon as we have students to teach. We must catch them in first and second year before attrition occurs. The interest gained in culture and global education activities may just keep them in our language courses longer.

Sample Activities

Activity 1—Social Class Structure Simulation (Crea, 8)

Randomly assign students to small groups by having them select color-coded cards. Unknown to students, each group represents a different social class as determined by race, religion, or any of a number of social factors. Divide students into groups based on a percentage of total students in the class. Percentages are determined by the social class content of the population of a country of the teacher's choosing. Each day students will participate in a small-group activity that can be completed in class. This can be any type of activity related to the other language content being studied in class. The type of activity is not critical to this simulation but rather the reward system is what is critical. No matter how well each group performs, points will be awarded according to a predetermined amount. Each group will always receive 100 percent of their possible points. The teacher does not inform students of the imbalance between groups in the awarding of points. The points represent the percentage of income the social group has of the total income of the country. For example, the following information may be used if one is studying income distribution in South Africa. (The red group represents the white population, the orange group represents the black population, the green group represents the "Coloured" or mulatto population, and the blue group the Asian population.)

Group	% of Class	Points Awarded
Red	15	70
Orange	72	20
Green	10	4
Blue	3	6

Source of information: Study Commission on U.S. Policy toward Southern Africa (16) and Chaliand and Rageau (5)[2]

At the end of each week the group totals their points and divides them equally among the group members. The points can be applied to their grades, used as extra credit, or used to buy treats or favors. It should not take too many days or weeks before the teacher is confronted with the injustice of the system. The teacher should be patient and wait for the students to figure out what has occurred. Students must *feel* the injustice in order for the full effect of the simulation to hit them. Only after the students have understood the nature of the injustice should the teacher explain to them what their groups represent: a particular racial group in South Africa (or any other country, race or type of social class as determined by the teacher).

The teacher can now lead the group to other activities concerning social injustice. For example, each group could complete a writing activity in which they must list reasons for maintaining, abolishing, or changing the point system. The entire class together then may wish to discuss what the new point system should be and try to reach some agreement. This will be a difficult task and should lead to some interesting discussion of the issues. A followup research activity could then be conducted on a number of African countries. The students should now be ready for the research as their social awareness has been raised and their interest stimulated in the issue.

Activity 2—The Heavy Burden of Debt (Franzen, 10)

As a preliminary assignment to this activity, students should make small flags of African countries. Students should also prepare book covers with the target language word for "debt" and "$10,000,000,000." Students should then select a card with the name of an African country and the amount of foreign debt the country owes. At this time students should cover old textbooks or other books with the book covers until the approximate amount of the debt is reached. Each book represents $10 billion.

The activity begins with the assignment that each student must carry the "debt" for their country around school that day. The length of time that each debt must be carried should be determined by the amount of resources the country has with which to pay the debt. For example, a country with a large debt will be very heavy, but if that country also has tremendous resources the student may only have to carry the debt for the first hour of the day. Another country with a very small debt may be an easy load, but the student would have to carry the debt for the entire day if the country has minimal resources. Students could research this information in advance or the teacher could provide the information on the card the students select at the beginning of the activity.

To add excitement to the activity, you may have additional students act as international police to ensure that the "countries" (which are easily identifiable due to the flags they are wearing) continue to carry the debt as assigned. As a followup activity, students should discuss their feelings about the burden of debt and resources necessary to pay debt. Due to the physical activity involved, a relatively difficult topic to conceptualize should become quite real for students and should stimulate both awareness and interest in the issue of foreign debt.

Conclusion

Global education is critical. Teaching about the target culture is not enough anymore. Neither our culture nor the target culture exist independently of each other or of the rest of the world but rather as significant parts of *interdependent* global society. Teachers must become involved in the effort to raise awareness of important issues among students studying languages. As a result, we will see students graduating from our programs not only able to speak another language but also able to interact in a knowledgeable and understanding manner with other peoples and cultures throughout the entire world.

Notes

1. The author acknowledges valuable contributions to this article by Jeffrey R. Mellgren, a scholar in the field of international relations.
2. Income distributions are approximations based on information found in the Report of the Study Commission on U.S. Policy toward Southern Africa.

References

1. Alger, Chadwick F. "Linking Town, Countryside and Legislature to the World."*International Studies Notes* 13 (1987):57–63.
2. Anderson, Lee. "The Century of the J Curve." *Principal* 6 (1981):12–15.
3. Becker, James M., and Lee Anderson. "Global Perspectives in the Social Studies." *Journal of Research and Development in Education* 13 (1980):82–91.
4. Brodbelt, Samuel. "Global Interdependence: Increasing Student Awareness." *Social Studies* 72 (1981):103–6.
5. Chaliand, Gerard, and Jean-Pierre Rageau. *A Strategic Atlas*. 2nd ed. New York: Harper & Row, 1985.
6. Cogan, John J. "Global Education: Opening Children's Eyes to the World." *Principal* 6 (1981):8–11.
7. Collins, H. Thomas. "East of Gibraltar, West of Japan: Questions and Answers about Global Education." *Principal* 6 (1981):16–19.
8. Crea, Joe Wild. "Social Classes: Income Distribution in Latin America." In Millie Park Mellgren, ed., *Cultural Activities for Contemporary Hispanic Issues*. Minneapolis: Alpha Print, 1987.
9. Fonte, Michael J. "Past as Prologue: A Current Issues Rationale for a Global Perspective." *Educational Research Quarterly* 8 (1983):108–11.
10. Franzen, Allen. "Foreign Debt." In Millie Park Mellgren, ed., *Cultural Activities for Contemporary Hispanic Issues*. Minneapolis: Alpha Print, 1987.
11. Kobus, Doni Kwolek. "The Developing Field of Global Education: A Review of the Literature." *Educational Research Quarterly* 8 (1983):21–28.
12. Lamy, Steven L. "Defining Global Education." *Educational Research Quarterly* 8 (1983):9–20.
13. Marker, Gerald W. "Global Education: An Urgent Claim on the Social Studies Curriculum." *Social Education* 41 (1977):12–19.
14. Remy, Richard. *International Learning and International Education in a Global Age*. Washington: National Council for Social Studies, 1975.
15. Seelye, H. Ned. *Teaching Culture: Strategies for Intercultural Communication*. Lincolnwood, IL: National Textbook Co., 1987.
16. Study Commission on U.S. Policy toward Southern Africa. *South Africa: Time Running Out*. Berkeley, CA: University of California Press, 1981.

5
The Civilization Course: Beyond the Textbook

Kathleen G. Boykin
Slippery Rock University, Slippery Rock, Pennsylvania

One of the essential areas of language instruction is the integration of culture into the curriculum. Indeed, culture is often spoken of as the fifth component of language acquisition, to be added to the traditional areas of listening, speaking, reading, and writing. At the college or university level, one or two culture/civilization courses are typically offered at the third level, frequently required of language majors, and taught in the target language. An examination of college catalogs reveals that the most common format is a two-semester sequence for French and German with the title "French (or German) Civilization and Culture I and II." In Spanish, one semester is devoted to Spain and a second to Latin America. There are, as might be expected, many other course titles and divisions, but the ones mentioned above are by far the most common.

There are, in addition, those institutions that offer the civilization courses in English rather than in the target language. The textbooks available in the target language from the major U.S. publishers are heavily oriented toward history with other chapters devoted to the great classics of art, literature, and music. There may be a smattering of other topics, but the bulk of the material presented is of this traditional format. There is often an attempt to address contemporary issues, but the textbooks are rapidly dated. Publishers of civilization/culture texts have yet to issue yearly updates as some encyclopedia publishers do. Nevertheless, if the textbook is followed with little deviation, the interested and conscientious student will emerge with an excellent background for the study of literature and for graduate study in the target language.

There are, however, certain problems inherent in a course that follows the textbook assiduously with little variation or addends. First, for one reason or another, many students are not particularly interested in history, art, or classical music. One certainly might argue that the student of today should be interested in those areas, that his/her "culture" is sadly lacking, etc. Nevertheless, the fact remains that courses with those same emphases are not likely to fill rapidly (unless, of course, they are required of a large number of students). Second, such courses do not familiarize the student with much of the contemporary culture of the country or peoples being studied. As mentioned previously, it is not possible for a textbook to remain current in recent events. A textbook cannot keep abreast of fads and unexpected events. Nevertheless, the civilization course should certainly include an awareness of the current reality. Indeed, future teachers and business leaders should be trained in consulting and utilizing sources of information that deal with current events of the target culture. Such behaviors will ultimately be more important than remembering much of the important historical information.

The traditional culture textbook presents the material and then asks the students to answer a series of questions. The student dutifully copies the answers from the appropriate section of the text. Frequently, there are vocabulary exercises and topics for discussion, but it is difficult for many third-year language students to carry on meaningful discussions in the target language. The vocabulary is often quite historical in nature and not very practical for everyday use and reinforcement.

Recently there has been an upsurge in the number of students entering teacher-education programs. In addition, student interest in pursuing careers in business remains strong. There are many students interested in international business, where language and business are combined. These two groups can benefit most from a modified civilization/culture course and the inclusion of culture in everyday language instruction. As a general rule, students rarely ask detailed questions about historical facts. They do, however, ask any number of more practical questions. The business students will someday be dealing with members of the target culture or will be asked to travel to the country being studied. A more viable course would include supplements to the textbook with examples of language in context and would reinforce the proficiency-oriented techniques now being used more and more at the beginning and intermediate levels.

In order to implement such a course, it is necessary to limit the amount of time spent on history. Another approach would be to choose a certain period to cover in depth and to skip lightly or greatly summarize other periods. The instructor of the course realizes that the history of the target country is relevant, fascinating, and extremely important, but many students do not share this point of view. The students frequently do not have the background the instructor wishes they had and often do not read as carefully as one might expect. Therefore, a discussion that the professor thinks will take only one class period can last for three. At that rate the Middle Ages might last until the midterm examination. If the course is to cover other topics and contemporary culture as well, these topics must be interspersed with or replace most of the historical doses. If the twentieth century is the most important period in the country's history, perhaps it should be discussed first. Too often the course is over and the professor never quite "got to" the twentieth century. Today's students, as a group, are more interested in the here and now than in the there and then. The civilization/culture course is an excellent vehicle for capitalizing on this interest.

In its revised format, the civilization and culture course is an effective motivator for continuing study of the language. In many smaller universities the culture/civilization course is currently offered once every two or three years. In others, the course is offered in English in hopes of attracting a wider audience. If the culture course is taught in a useful and interesting manner, it is possible to offer it in the target language on a regular basis.

Schools might even want to consider a civilization course as a replacement for the third-year conversation-composition course. There are ready-made topics for reading, writing, listening, and speaking activities. It is not necessary to find ways to include the culture component, for that is the focus of the course. In a civilization course there are always opportunities for narration and description in every tense. There are many situations with complications that can be introduced as students learn to negotiate their way through the target culture. Advanced students can give their opinions on a variety of topics and defend them to the rest of the class. At the same time, the student is learning valuable information and practicing useful material.

Universities without regular large enrollments in the civilization course should give special consideration to abandoning the traditional approach. Some may argue that a student who will probably take only one civilization course must have a particular one. Others may feel strongly that a course that does not examine in detail the various elements of the war for independence in each South American country is not a "real" civilization course. However, it is probable that few students remember many of the fascinating historical details, which instructors are accustomed to present at a fairly rapid pace so that all of them will be covered in the time available. Students are more apt to retain global concepts that have been presented in relation to something they understand. A revised course with more communicative activities related to aspects of the contemporary civilization will seem more relevant and interesting to them.

As a further aid to increasing enrollments, a language department should consider offering two or more courses that are independent of each other, such as "French Civilization and Culture" and "The Civilization and Cultures of French-Speaking Countries." Spanish professors have long been forced to deal with the impossibility of presenting the entire civilization of several countries in one semester. The more courses offered, the more opportunities are available to the interested nonmajor who refuses to study literature. It is possible to divide the French civilization still further with courses on French Africa and French Canada. In Spanish, there are usually courses on Spain and Latin America. Latin America can be divided into Mexico, Central America, the Caribbean, and South America. A course dealing specifically with Hispanics in the U.S. is both practical and beneficial to students who will be working daily with this growing segment of the U.S. population. In German similar divisions are feasible. Another possibility is to include just one course in the catalog, but to offer different topics every semester on a rotating basis with students' having the possibility of repeating the same course (on a different topic) for credit. Different titles are better for the students' records, however.

Whenever possible, different professors should teach the civilization courses so that the students get a choice of perspectives. It is preferable that the structure and orientation of each course vary. In this way the students will be in an entirely different course rather than in very similar courses with slight variation in subject matter. One course could emphasize dealing with the people, another could stress the role of history in shaping the current political and economic situation, a third could deal with the culture as revealed through the media. One professor might prefer to teach with extensive use of videos; another might prefer readings as a basis for interpreting the culture; a third might choose a multiple eclectic approach.

At Slippery Rock University (where only 10 percent of the student body is subject to the language requirement), the restructuring of the civilization courses in Spanish has resulted in enrollments of 35 to 45 students per semester in one of four courses that are offered on a rotating basis. The courses are offered in Spanish with only occasional materials in English. The college language requirement is to complete Basic Spanish III, so students must pass through the intermediate level before reaching the civilization classes. The literature class at the same level (required of majors) is offered only every other semester and has about 10 to 12 students enrolled. The typical student at our medium-sized public institution does not appreciate the value of the study of literature. The civilization courses as now presented seem to be "relevant" and useful to business majors, future elementary and secondary teachers, social-work majors, and also Spanish majors. The Spanish section has been successful in generating considerable enthusiasm for minoring in Spanish, and the culture/civilization courses are a popular choice for Spanish minors.

Supplementary Materials

The topics listed below are only a few of the many that can be integrated into civilization and culture courses.

Current events.   Too often the students view the target country as something long ago and far away. It is easy to forget that history is still being made. One technique is to have a portion of time every week devoted to the news of that week. Sources include the international edition of a newspaper in the target language, such as *El País* from Spain, or a newsmagazine, such as France's *L'Express*. The professor can select the items and distribute them to the students or can present the items orally with a guide. The news items are an excellent source of contemporary vocabulary. In addition, it is interesting to discuss how the news (of the Olympics or the U.S. presidential election, for example) is presented differently in the target culture than in the United States. Discussions of the differences in points of view of the two cultures and the historical background of the situations can follow. The Spanish opposition to U.S. bases in Spain, for example, can be related to Spain's long history of independence and neutrality. Students can also be asked to choose a news item on which to report either orally or as a written assignment. At some point, the information and the selected vocabulary should be tested.

Radio and TV.   A school with access to a satellite dish or to other foreign language programming should include "live" broadcasts of current events. The professor may wish to tape the program in advance and then ask the students to listen for selected topics. Radio programs can be dealt with in much the same way, but comprehension is more difficult without pictures. A unit on TV is generally of great interest to the students. In the weekly newsmagazines from the foreign country can be found a section with the TV listings. Again, the students can be given a worksheet to lead them to certain discoveries, such as how many channels are available, how many hours a day the programs are on, whether or not cable is available, what kinds of movies are shown, and how recent they are, etc. The professor can send the student to search out the answers in magazines from a variety of issues or can distribute a copy of one week's schedule. The information gathered can be used as a basis for discussion of any number of topics, such as the government's role in the TV industry, the American influence in the target culture, the type and quality of programming and possible reasons for it, the presence or absence of censorship, or the manner in which time appears on schedules (20.10 for 8:10, e.g.). Thus, a seemingly trivial topic (but one of considerable student interest) can be used as a basis for presenting several more meaningful topics.

Products.   A typical unit on products could include a commercial slide/tape program supplemented by additional slides either purchased or taken by the professor. Samples of the products mentioned can be displayed. The professor can bring in all the souvenirs gathered from numerous trips abroad. Seeing the product is much more effective than just reading about it in a book.

As part of a discussion of the various types of sherry, it is very effective to bring in three bottles, pour the contents into three sherry glasses, and let the students observe the differences in color and aroma. University regulations undoubtedly preclude actually tasting the difference, but the concept is still imprinted on the students' minds. This discussion will also keep future businessmen from ordering a glass of sherry as an accompaniment to their steak and leads into a discussion of the similarities and differences in drinking habits. Thus, one area can lead very naturally to another. A further ramification of the sherry presentation is an explanation of the origin of the word and how the Spanish language has evolved in spelling and pronunciation of the sound now represented by *j*. At this point a discussion of drinking attitudes and habits in general can naturally occur.

In addition to the more typical products purchased by tourists or associated with the country, those products that are important but not so colorful must also be included. Many students are unaware that these countries are competing on the world market with items other than beer steins, miniature Eiffel Towers, and dolls in flamenco dresses. The unit on products can include a discussion of the country's economy, the reasons for the state it is in, the workforce and laws governing it, the problems faced currently and in the past, and the reasons behind said problems.

The use of commercials from radio, TV, or magazines will also add to the students' vocabulary, oral comprehension skills, and awareness of the target culture. Here again the U.S. influence can be discussed. Students can be asked to compare the focus for selling certain products in different countries. A discussion on values can fall in here also. Is there advertising for alcohol and cigarettes? Are the ads more subdued or more sensual? The possibilities for areas of discussion are many. The student of the 80s is media-oriented. Rather than lamenting the addiction to mass media, the professor can capitalize on it.

Food.   One of the most popular topics is the food unit, which may include practicing eating European style in the cafeteria, peeling an orange or a banana with a knife and fork, cleaning fresh squid, or making tortillas or crêpes from scratch. In one two-hour period, it was possible for a Mexican civilization class to prepare, eat, and clean up a Mexican dinner for the 38 students in the class—all in the classroom. The class enjoyed tacos prepared with fresh tortillas, enchiladas, refried beans, ceviche, nonalcoholic sangría, Christmas Eve salad, guacamole, chicken and rice, and other delicacies. With organization all things are possible.

The food unit is a point of departure for discussions or role playing based on eating schedules, forbidden or unpopular foods, etiquette and other tips for future student and business travelers. Food is another area in which to stress that U.S. customs are not exclusively the "right" ones. The economic history can also be a part of a unit on food. Mention can be made of which invaders were responsible for the introduction of which foods and why. Students can discuss the pros and cons of installing

American fast-food restaurants all over the world. The tangents are at the discretion of the professor.

Art.   Rather than presenting a comprehensive view of all the major artists of the country, it is more effective to concentrate on a few very important artists and to show students how to recognize the works of those artists. Show slides and video tapes. Test with pictures and slides. Don't include too many. Assign students to write brief reports on the life and/or work of an artist of their choice. When applicable, relate the artists' works to the history and literature of the period.

Music.   Again, concentrate on only a few. Play the music. Teach typical dances. Don't stop with the classical musicians. Add the modern popular singers. Play the tapes you bought on your last trip. Look at the list of best-selling LP's in the newsmagazine. Here again, you can talk about the American influence and the fact that other cultures listen to music from many different countries. There are videos available in this area also.

Transportation.   A presentation of the country's most common means of transportation can include many practical details, such as the different classes on trains, buses, and subways; how to read a timetable; the vocabulary needed for train travel; the laws governing automobiles and licenses; how to read the international signs; and the price of cars and gasoline. Again, the presentation of one fact can lead to many other areas. When students see small European cars or old American-style cars in Mexico, they do not realize the economic implications behind their observations. It is surprising to them what percentage of a person's income must be used in order to purchase a car or gasoline for it. The tax structure on automobiles and the licensing system are also of interest. The price of gasoline can lead into a mention of the metric system, which in turn can lead to a discussion of clothing sizes. The key is to decide what cultural items will be included in the course and where they will best fit.

Other Possibilities.   Other topics might include education, particular folk customs, religion, the role of women, problems facing the country, important figures, and the organization of the government. The topics and organization of the course will vary continually. The professor, therefore, must remain current and spend some time organizing the supplemental materials.

Sources of Materials

Commercial Sources.   Several publishers have materials available that emphasize the more popular aspects of the culture. It is only necessary to visit the displays at a large conference or peruse the catalogs to find many items and programs of interest.

Videos.   In addition to the exciting possibilities for using actual television programs originating from the target country, presentation of commercial videos is always of interest to the TV generation. At present the videos available are new enough not to suffer from the dating so evident in many slide or film programs. A video is an effective way to present the geography of the country. Tours of the Prado and the Louvre are available on videocassette. Other video programs examine the ancient civilizations of the Americas. More and more programs will be available in the future, and the language professional will be able to be more discriminating. More and more programs are being made available with commentary in the target language. In this way the student is able to practice listening comprehension in a relatively nonthreatening manner. Students feel more secure when they are able to see what they are hearing. The video can be stopped to point out items of interest and it can be played again. The video can be put in the language laboratory so that the student can go back to watch and listen again. (It is possible to have an earphone jack added to a TV monitor for a very low cost.) Videocassettes are also available for rental at a very low cost from large universities and other rental outlets.

The teacher-made video is another possibility for inclusion in the culture course. In addition to videos made in the foreign country, a video of interviews with exchange students and other foreign nationals can be made and kept for those semesters when no one is available for a live presentation. The teacher-made video has the advantage that it can easily be duplicated and shared with other teachers.

There are also many programs on commercial television that are extremely useful in the classroom. Many of these are only short segments but can be very effective to illustrate a certain point. The fact that the information was actually presented on television here in the United States somehow makes it seem more believable or more important to the students. Some universities have structured entire courses around culture as presented in the various media. Writing a paper about a video program or movie shown on video can replace the more traditional report written to interpret a book or short story.

Slides.   The slide has not yet disappeared completely and still has its advantages. It is still easier to carry a 35mm camera than it is to carry around a video camera, but this advantage may not last much longer. It is often more discrete to take a picture, especially with a telephoto lens, than it is to make a video. Slides can be used effectively for pictures in which the action is not important. Slides of great monuments can be very successful. Slides can be used for identifying architectural features. Food can be presented via slides.

The instructor taking slides should remember to take slides of those everyday items that may not appear in a commercial production. Students are interested in clothing displays in a store window. They like to see posters announcing performances of rock groups. The marquee of a theater showing an American film with the title in the target language is always an attention grabber. Displays of food in the supermarket and cases of beer waiting to be drunk are always popular. With a macro lens it is also relatively simple to make your own slides of ticket stubs, subway tickets, magazine ads, money, etc. Rather than having a certain day set aside for slides, the slides should be integrated into the units being presented. It is possible to show only a few slides at a time. It is not necessary to spend the whole period every time slides are shown.

Clippings.   The civilization instructor should keep an organized file of culture-related topics. Whenever an article appears on a certain topic, such as the role of women, education, abortion, popular music, drugs, housing, social security, the penal code, the price of gasoline, or any number of other topics, the article or a slip with the information on it and the date should be placed into the file (after being read, of course). This requires considerable organization, but it also enables the instructor to become very knowledgeable on multiple aspects of contemporary civilization. These articles can be found in American magazines and newspapers, in foreign publications, and in material distributed to foreign language teachers. Each file can become a possible topic for discussion in class or to supplement statements in the text or in a video program. Copies of the material in a certain folder can be distributed to students for reports to the class. The student is given the opportunity to work with authentic material, to organize it, and to give an oral or written presentation, thus reinforcing language skills.

Realia.   Most of the realia collected during trips abroad can be incorporated into the class in some way. It is also essential that the foreign language instructor have the culture class in mind when traveling to the target country. The Spanish system of dealing with last names becomes more meaningful when the student tries to fill out an application blank asking for *apellidos*. Brochures passed out by political parties can aid in describing the political process at work in the country. Reading the train schedule from the published book has an air of authenticity. High school teachers have been collecting these items for years.

Summary

By supplementing the textbook through the introduction of units related to contemporary culture, by deemphasizing the traditional linear historical approach, by adding a variety of student-centered activities, and by adapting the course to the needs and interests of the student, civilization and culture courses will be a vibrant and popular component of the curriculum. Through the use of videos, realia, newspapers, magazines, and other authentic sources, the students are more apt to see the relevance of the material being taught. By concentrating more on the relationship of the past to the present and on the effect that history has had on the current reality, the civilization course becomes more exciting and, at the same time, more useful to the student. Such a course better prepares the student who will be traveling to the country or working with members of the target culture. The use of multiple sources for information will sensitize the students to the availability of these sources and may inspire them to remain current. And, a revitalized civilization course can be a source of increased enrollment. Thus, the civilization/culture class becomes an integral component in a proficiency-oriented curriculum.

References

1. Allen, Wendy W. "Toward Cultural Proficiency," in Alice C. Omaggio, ed., *Proficiency, Curriculum, Articulation: The Ties That Bind*. Middlebury, VT: The Northeast Conference (1985):137–66.
2. Brooks, Nelson. "Teaching Culture in the Foreign Language Classroom." *Foreign Language Annals* 1 (1968):204–17.
3. Griffin, Robert J. "Using Current Magazines as a Resource for Teaching Culture." *Hispania* 70 (1987):479–84.
4. Lafayette, Robert C., and Renate A. Schulz. *Teaching Culture: Strategies and Techniques*. Language in Education: Theory and Practice Series, No. 11. Washington, DC: Center for Applied Linguistics, 1978.
5. Medley, Frank W., Jr., and Carmen Villegas Rogers. "Language with a Purpose: Using Authentic Materials in the Foreign Language Classroom." *Foreign Language Annals* 21 (1988):467–78.
6. Omaggio, Alice C. *Teaching Language in Context, Proficiency-Oriented Instruction*. Boston, M: Heinle & Heinle, 1986.
7. Seelye, H. Ned. *Teaching Culture: Strategies for Intercultural Communication*. Lincolnwood, IL: National Textbook Company, 1976.

6
Classroom Activities: A Task-Analysis Approach[1]

Diane W. Birckbichler
The Ohio State University, Columbus

The concept of methodology as an organizing principle for the teaching of second languages is undergoing rigorous scrutiny. A method presents to the teacher a well-conceptualized and well-organized set of principles of language learning; these theories guide teachers in short-term and long-term planning and in the day-to-day selection of activities in the classroom. Despite the usefulness of a methods framework, this approach to language teaching poses several problems. For example, adherents of a particular method may be imbued with evangelical zeal and try to convert all teachers to the one true way. Maley (cited in Dubin and Olshtain, 3) describes the difficulties of guru-centered methods where "the approach gathers around it a ritual set of procedures, a priesthood (complete with initiatory courses necessary to license practice) and a body of holy writ and commentary" (p. 65). The closed nature of many methods is also a problem. Stern (11), for example, sees a method as relatively fixed and inflexible and therefore not open to or perhaps resistant to change. He also notes that a method may overemphasize a particular aspect of second language learning and view it as the central aspect of language learning at the expense of other (and perhaps more important) characteristics of the teaching/learning process. Asher's (1) emphasis on the imperative in his Total Physical Response approach exemplifies this tendency. Finally, the focus on methodology has emphasized primarily the teaching act and has often failed to consider student needs and individual differences.

Because of these limitations, the idea of methodology is generally being replaced by a growing eclecticism, i.e., the selection of techniques and approaches from a variety of sources. At the present time, methods seem much less important than theories of language learning, student learning styles and strategies, and the selection of activities that are conducive to student learning and congruent with program goals. Rivers (10) in her description of the "eclectic approach" distinguishes between a true eclecticist and a drifter. A drifter adopts new techniques without care and thought; the eclecticist, on the other hand, is flexible in his/her choice of methods and thoughtful in the selection of materials.[2]

An Alternative: A Task-Analysis Approach

As is evidenced by Rivers's distinction between a true eclecticist and the irresponsible drifter, an eclectic approach does not mean a lack of responsibility on the part of the teacher nor does it imply the random and capricious use of activities and techniques. Rather, it suggests the need to find alternative ways to evaluate our approaches to foreign language teaching. Omaggio (7, 8), suggests that methods can be evaluated for the presence or absence of proficiency-oriented characteristics. As her analysis notes, a method such as the Grammar-Translation Method would be low on proficiency characteristics, whereas the Direct Method, for example, would be a more proficiency-oriented method.

Swaffar, Arens, and Morgan (12) propose task hierarchy as an alternative to the concept of methodology. In their research, they found that the methods they investigated (a comprehension-based approach and a four-skills approach) used basically the same classroom activities. What differentiated them was not the presence or absence of particular activities but the order in which activities are used (i.e., their priority in a task hierarchy) and their frequency of use. Although the focus of their research is still closely linked to methodology, their concept of task hierarchy differs from a methodological approach in its insistence on the examination of how often activities are actually used in the learning sequences implied by certain methods rather than on their hypothetical use.

Another alternative to a methods approach is task analysis, in which teachers examine different dimensions of classroom tasks, assess the degree to which activities possess certain characteristics, and determine to what extent each activity contributes to desired learning outcomes. A set of possible dimensions to use in this type of task analysis could include items such as the following: (1) mechanical/communicative; (2) classroom/realistic; (3) structured/open-ended; (4) analysis/synthesis; (5) passive/active; (6) pedagogical/authentic. These categories are descriptive and are not meant to be evaluative. In other words, the lower ends of the different dimensions do not necessarily indicate negative ratings, because the activity needs to be examined not only in relationship to course goals but also in light of the activity's place in a learning sequence. A structured mechanical activity, for instance, does not have negative connotations when viewed in light of the need to provide structured practice at early levels of language instruction. It would be judged differently if it were the culminating activity in a course where oral fluency was the goal. Definitions and examples of these characteristics are given below.

1. The mechanical/communicative dimension (Paulston and Selekman, 9) allows assessment of the degree to which an activity is a mechanical (i.e., with little or no attention to meaning required), meaningful (i.e., the student must attend to the meaning of the language to complete the task), or communicative (in which students transmit their own messages). Given the current focus on proficiency and communicative language use, it is important that teachers and materials writers be able to make these distinctions.

2. Classroom/realistic refers to the realism of the activity. Is the task representative of the classroom or is it one that would be performed in the second language culture? Galloway (4) describes authentic tasks as "those which invite the learner to do what would be done, in much the way it would be done, by native speakers of the language" (p. 50). She contrasts classroom discussion of a weather report (questions on all aspects of the report) with real-life usage of the weather report to make decisions about what clothing to wear the next day. The relative realism of pedagogical tasks can also vary. For example, a structured conversation format where questions are provided is less realistic than a more open-ended activity that asks students to talk about their weekend plans. Role plays, because they simulate situations that might occur in the culture, are closer to the realistic end of the continuum.

3. The structured/open-ended dimension allows the assessment of the amount and degree of structure in a given activity. A composition task in which questions are provided is more structured than an open-ended composition in which only the topic is given. A task that asks students to read a paragraph and answer predetermined

questions is more structured than a task that requires students to read a newspaper article and prepare a short abstract of the content. Early in an instructional sequence, students might need, for example, more highly structured oral activities; at later stages continued reliance on this structure may well impede the development of the student's ability to speak spontaneously.

4. Analysis refers to the degree to which the student analyzes and describes the language; synthesis relates to the extent to which the student is required to put the language together. Some examples of analysis tasks are identification of cognates in a reading passage, explanation of the grammatical function of underlined words in a paragraph, and identification of errors in a composition. Tasks where synthesis is the dominating activity include writing compositions, oral communicative activities, reading or listening to passages and answering questions, etc. A task that asks students to identify the different verb tenses in a paragraph is a highly analytical task. A task requiring a written résumé of a reading is closer to the synthesis end of the continuum, and although analysis of the material is involved in comprehension, the dominant process is the synthesis of information.

5. The passive/active dimension assesses the degree of student involvement in classroom tasks. For example, listening to a lecture on a grammatical point where no followup questions are asked and where there is no assessment of comprehension is a potentially passive task; this same task becomes more active if students are asked questions as the lecture progresses. Although students may well be attentive (or at least appear to pay attention) during a lecture, assessment of comprehension encourages student attention.

Thus, the presence of followup tasks that test student comprehension of material is essential in determining the degree to which a task is active or passive.

An additional factor is the nature of the student involvement; although students may well be actively involved in pronouncing second language words, time might be more profitably spent asking students to use these words in dialogs that they make up and present to the class.

6. Pedagogical/authentic differentiates between materials that have been prepared specifically for classroom use by the teacher or

materials writers and those that are authentic documents from the second language culture. In between these two ends of the continuum, one also finds variations such as "simulated authentic discourse" described by Geddes and White (cited in Omaggio, 8) as "language produced for pedagogical purposes, but which exhibits features that have a high probability of occurrence in genuine acts of communication" (p. 128). According to Omaggio, teacher talk or comprehensible input with emphasis on a simplified code, increased use of known vocabulary, slower pronunciation, and intentional paraphrasing of ideas to help ensure comprehension is an example of simulated authentic discourse.

Using these dimensions in the analysis of classroom tasks and activities encourages teachers to focus on the processes involved in language learning and to examine what the task demands of classroom activities *actually* are rather than to focus on what they think or hope students are doing. Research by Hosenfeld (6) revealed that students (despite what teachers and materials writers thought) were not looking at the meaning of words as they completed pattern drills. Instead, they were looking for a quick and efficient way to complete the drill. For instance, in sentences requiring the use of the pronoun *y* in French, students looked only for the noun that was to be replaced by *y* and not at the whole sentence.

Using Task Analysis

Task-analysis exercise can be used in several ways. First, teachers can examine more closely the actual processing demands of classroom tasks, thus becoming more sensitive to the potential of classroom activities. The relative usefulness of pedagogical and authentic activities can be discussed and the place of classroom versus realistic tasks examined. Teachers can also judge how effective each activity is in reaching course goals. If a course or program emphasizes one skill, activities that emphasize that skill can be identified and teachers asked to first assess the task's characteristics and then to prioritize them in terms of how useful they are in reaching course goals. For example, a program that focuses on reading would want to minimize (but not necessarily exclude totally) the use of teacher-prepared readings and would choose instead to emphasize authentic materials.

A task-analysis approach can also be useful in teacher training programs. For example, preservice teachers could profit greatly from an examination of classroom activities and their contributions to course goals. A sample task-analysis worksheet is included in the appendix. This worksheet can be used in several ways. Students or workshop participants can be asked to identify the activities along a single dimension or rate them along the six dimensions given. It should be noted that tasks are evaluated on a continuum rather than simply for the presence or absence of a certain characteristic. Not all tasks need be analyzed, and other activities can be substituted for those given on the worksheet. The discussion that follows the categorization of activities along the different dimensions is essential; the discussions might include topics such as (1) frequency of use, (2) possible reasons for use, (3) contribution to course goals, (4) individual student differences or class characteristics, and (5) possible modifications. Equally important is the participants' modification of activities to conform more closely to course goals.

For example, the first item on the sample worksheet asks students to analyze an activity in which the teacher explains a grammar rule in English to the class; students are subsequently asked to paraphrase the grammar rule. First, although the activity is not communicative, it is not totally mechanical either, since students are required to pay attention to what is said in order to rephrase the rule later. The task is designed for classroom use and is relatively structured in that few options are given. The task is more analytical than synthetic and although not totally passive (students are required to indicate their understanding of the rule), the task does not show that they are able to transfer their knowledge of the rule to situations where the second language is used. The content of the activity is clearly pedagogical rather than authentic. Additional discussion can clarify the usefulness (or lack thereof) of the activity; if used infrequently and briefly, a task such as this, although not ideal, is not necessarily a problem. If, however, the teacher uses such activities frequently and thus deprives students of the opportunity to use the second language in more realistic situations, then the task needs to be eliminated and/or modified. Modifications might include assigning the study of the grammar rule for homework or changing the students' followup task; instead of paraphrasing the rule, they might be asked to create sentences that illustrate the rule or demonstrate their comprehension in a grammar drill or communicative activity.

Another task on the worksheet (No. 27) asks students to translate an article from a second language newspaper about recent elections in that culture. Clearly, the activity is not mechanical, because students are processing the meaning of the article; and although analysis is involved in completing the translation, the predominant activity is synthesizing the information for the translation. The students are actively involved in this classroom-oriented task. Because no structure or help is given to aid the students in their translation of the article, the task is nearer the open-ended range of the structured/open-ended dimension. Teachers might well question frequent use of this activity in the development of reading skills as it encourages a focus on detail rather than on understanding the main ideas of a text. On the other hand, some students, especially those who are impulsive and not attentive enough to detail, may profit from such an activity. Teachers hoping to increase the number of realistic, real-world activities that they include in their lesson plans might decide to modify the activity; students could be asked to give the translation to their world-history teacher for use in his or her class or to publish it in the school newspaper.

Actual (or simulated) lesson plans can also be analyzed for the presence or absence of certain characteristics. Preservice teachers often have difficulty in identifying actual rather than desired contributions of an activity and in understanding the relationship of the task to that lesson plan in particular and to course goals in general. For example, preservice teachers might not realize the importance of planning followup activities to ensure that students are "on task" rather than assuming that they are. Students may seem to be listening to the teacher's lecture on the second language culture; if, however, they are not required to demonstrate comprehension, teacher assumptions about their attentiveness are still hypothetical. They might also be unaware of the preponderance of a certain type of activity in their lesson plans; task analysis of their lesson plans would clearly demonstrate the characteristics of the tasks they have chosen to include.

Conclusion

Higgs (5) described the relative comfort of language teaching earlier in this century: "How comfortable it must have been teaching foreign languages during the first half of this century! Few prolonged controversies over goals, methods, materials, or assessment procedures disturbed the professional calm" (p. 8). Additional comfort was later provided within the rather strict confines of different methodologies. An individual trained in ALM methodology, for example, did not have to ask questions about classroom procedures—those answers had already been supplied. The person trained to teach a "pure" direct method did not have to question whether to translate in the classroom: the method itself would preclude such activity.

Today, teachers still have many questions about language learning and teaching. With the waning importance of methodologies and the ready guidelines that they provided, teachers will have to find alternative ways to assess the usefulness of classroom activities and their contributions to learning goals. The task-analysis procedures described here provide one way to judge the effectiveness of tasks and techniques; others will certainly be found. What is clear is the importance of carefully establishing course goals and then examining the contribution of classroom activities, materials, and techniques to these goals. In this way, teachers will respond more clearly to student and program needs rather than adhere to methodologies that may not be appropriate for their students, that may be congruent with only one narrow way of viewing language learning or learners, or that reflect idiosyncratic or "gimmicky" approaches to second language learning.

Notes

1. This paper is a revised version of a workshop given at the ACTFL/DOD Baltimore Symposium, 1987.
2. Excellent summaries and description of methods are found in Benseler and Schulz (2), Omaggio (7, 8), Rivers (10), and Stern (11).
3. The sample worksheet is adapted from a worksheet handed out by Swaffar et al. at the 1987 ACTFL Symposium in Baltimore.

References

1. Asher, James J., JoAnne Kusudo, and Rita de la Torre. "Learning a Second Language through Commands: The Second Field Test." *Modern Language Journal* 58 (1974):24–32.
2. Benseler, David P., and Renate A. Schulz. "Methodological Trends in College Foreign Language Instruction." *Modern Language Journal* 64 (1980):88–96.
3. Dubin, Fraida, and Elite Olshtain. *Course Design. Developing Programs and Materials for Foreign Language Learning.* Cambridge, Eng.: Cambridge University Press, 1986.
4. Galloway, Vicki. "From Defining to Developing Proficiency: A Look at the Decisions," pp. 25–75 in Heidi Byrnes and Michael Canale, eds., *Defining and Developing Proficiency: Guidelines, Implementations, and Concepts.* The ACTFL Foreign Language Education Series, vol. 17. Lincolnwood, IL: National Textbook Company, 1987.
5. Higgs, Theodore V. "Language Acquisition and Language Learning: A Plea for Syncretism." *Modern Language Journal* 69 (1985):8–14.

6. Hosenfeld, Carol. "The New Student Role: Individual Differences and Implications for Instruction," pp. 129–68 in Gilbert A. Jarvis, ed., *Perspective: A New Freedom*. The ACTFL Foreign Language Education Series, vol. 7. Lincolnwood, IL: National Textbook Company, 1975.
7. Omaggio, Alice. "Methodology in Transition. The New Focus on Proficiency." *Modern Language Journal* 67 (1983):330–41.
8. ———. *Teaching Language in Context*. Boston: Heinle and Heinle, 1986.
9. Paulston, C. B., and H. R. Selekman. "Interactive Activities in the Foreign Language Classroom or How to Grow a Tulip-Rose." *Foreign Language Annals* 9 (1976):248–54.
10. Rivers, Wilga M. *Teaching Foreign Language Skills*. 2nd ed. Chicago: University of Chicago Press, 1981.
11. Stern, H. H. *Fundamental Concepts of Language Teaching*. Oxford, Eng.: Oxford University Press, 1983.
12. Swaffar, Janet K., Katherine Arens, and Martha Morgan. "Teacher Classroom Practices: Redefining Methods as Task Hierarchy." *Modern Language Journal* 61 (1982):24–33.

Appendix[3]

Evaluate each of the following classroom activities using the rating scales given below. You may evaluate the activities along all dimensions or choose to focus on one of the dimensions below in your evaluation.

Mechanical					Communicative
	1	2	3	4	5
Classroom					Realistic
	1	2	3	4	5
Structured					Open-ended
	1	2	3	4	5
Analysis					Synthesis
	1	2	3	4	5
Passive					Active
	1	2	3	4	5
Pedagogical					Authentic
	1	2	3	4	5

1. The teacher explains a point of grammar in English to the class; students subsequently paraphrase the rule in English.
2. Students rearrange or indicate the order of a scrambled list of sentences to summarize what they have read or heard.
3. Students read or listen to authentic texts with instructions to ignore difficult or potentially frustrating parts and to prepare recall protocols of the passage (e.g., write down in English as much as they can remember).
4. Students take dictation in L2: They either write down entire sentences or fill in blanks with words, phrases, or sentences omitted from the dictation, which is a recombination passage of previously learned material.
5. Students are asked to read a teacher-prepared text and analyze the grammatical function of selected words.

6. Students are asked to listen to a short, teacher-prepared selection (excerpted and adapted from a radio broadcast) and to answer short informational questions about the passage.

7. Students are asked to read a short, teacher-prepared selection and to underline synonymous expressions they find in it.

8. Students scan authentic texts, looking for answers to specific questions and ignoring irrelevant information (e.g., read results of elections and look only for the winner of a particular Senate seat).

9. Students skim authentic texts to answer a very general, inferential question such as "What is the tone of the article: humorous, serious, sarcastic, etc.?" or "What was the intended audience of the article?"

10. Students read a teacher-prepared text and find and categorize all verbs according to their tense.

11. Students read an article from a second language magazine and underline loan words and cognates.

12. Before reading an article from a second language newspaper, students preview the content by discussing the title, paragraph subheads, topic sentences, and a set of keywords.

13. Students carry out commands given to them by the teacher or other students (Go to Reginald, take his books, put them on Susan's desk, jump on your left foot back to your desk).

14. Students are asked to practice repeating textbook dialogs in groups of two.

15. Students pronounce lists of words containing selected sounds in the foreign language.

16. Students complete oral pattern drills that consist of isolated, random sentences illustrating a particular grammar point.

17. Students write letters to businesses or government offices in the second language country to obtain information for personal use (e.g., job possibilities, travel information).

18. Students are asked to role-play situations that might occur in the L2 culture (looking for a room, ordering a meal).

19. Students are asked to debate controversial topics.

20. Students are asked to identify and correct the errors in the compositions they have written.

21. Students are asked to complete fill-in-the-blank written grammar exercises where verbs to use are given in parentheses after each sentence.

22. Students are asked to fill in the blanks in a paragraph with a word or phrase that fits the context.

23. The teacher presents a lecture on an aspect of the L2 culture.

24. Students are asked to apply their cultural knowledge to authentic documents from the L2 culture (e.g., categorize a newspaper's editorial orientation based on assessment of its content).

25. Students work in groups of two and are given cards with prepared personal questions that they ask each other.

26. Students are asked to practice a particular grammar point by translating sentences from English to L2.

27. Students are asked to give a word-for-word translation of an authentic text about the results of recent elections in the L2 culture in order to assess their comprehension of the text.

28. Students complete listening discrimination tasks (e.g., positive/negative, present/past, statement/interrogative).

29. Students use prepared questions to write short paragraphs about topics of a personal nature (e.g., what they did last weekend, what their summer plans are).

30. Students are asked to keep journals in which they record their daily activities.

31. Students are asked to write résumés of conversations they have with other students.

32. Students are asked to take notes of a recorded lecture (taped in a classroom in the L2 culture) on an academic topic.

33. Students read the entertainment page of an L2 newspaper in order to decide what to do over the weekend.

7
You and Your Textbook: Legal Separation—Not a Divorce

Alan Garfinkel
Purdue University, Indiana
Mary Beth Berghian
South Bend Community School Corporation, Indiana

Only the very smallest minority of American secondary-school foreign language classes today operates without the aid of a textbook of one kind or another. It is clear that textbooks are of immeasurable help to the classroom teacher of foreign languages. Inappropriate use of textbooks, however, can also stifle innovation and variety. This article proposes to illustrate some of the problems caused by inappropriate use of textbooks, to suggest successful ways to use a textbook, to discuss the acceptance and rejection of these paths to success in the use of a textbook, and, thus, to show that the problems caused by inappropriate use may not always be as insoluble as is sometimes thought.

Become the proverbial "fly on the wall" and eavesdrop on parts of several conversations that may very well have taken place in your own school:

Case 1 (Principal's Office)

PRINCIPAL: The reason I wanted to speak with you this afternoon, Mr. Jones, is that while observing your class, I noted that you have completed five chapters of your text while the other French teachers have apparently completed nine. Is there a reason?

Case 2 (Teachers' Workroom)

LOUNGE LIZARD: What chapter of the book are you on? I heard that Mary Jane is three chapters ahead of us. I don't have to tell you why, do I?

(Later that day)

L.L. (to another colleague): Mary Jane just got back from that whatchamacallit Mid-States Conference on the Teaching of Foreign Languages. Those conferences are okay. I went to one myself a few years ago, but, you know, those professor types that speak there never seem to realize that there's just not enough time in a school year to cover all we have to cover. I mean some of that innovative stuff is okay, but. . . we just can't get to it. Besides, if I hear the word *proficiency* one more time, I swear I'm going to be ill right here on the lounge floor.

Case 3 (Parents' Night Meeting Room)

PARENT: I'm so tired of hearing Melinda complain about Spanish class.
FRIEND: What do you mean?
PARENT: She keeps saying that it's the same boring stuff they did last year.
FRIEND: Maybe you should talk to the teacher before Melinda drops the class.

Case 4 (Students' Lunchroom)

STUDENT: How's Spanish?
FRIEND: Well, you know.
STUDENT: What happened?
FRIEND: Well, we walk into class and he goes, "Open your books to chapter 1."
STUDENT: So?
FRIEND: Well, so I go, "We did this already." And he's like soooo paranoid.

The problem these vignettes illustrate is clear. There are various interpretations of what it means to have accomplished the work of a given level of language instruction. Some people think that such accomplishment means having memorized or otherwise completely absorbed every word of every page of a textbook. Some do not. Textbooks are to be used like maps, not prescriptions. One can carry the analogy further and remember that in making a trip with a map, one selects the roadways that lead to the declared destination (or behavioral outcomes of teaching).

To accomplish our departure, standards for using the textbook in curriculum design are proposed herein. These standards can allow teachers to use the textbook in planning for teaching, but they must also allow for leaving out parts of the textbook and adding materials from other, more innovative sources such as conference handouts, reference books, games, worksheets, and authentic materials that may assist in leading to the accomplishment of the work one sets out to do.

Second, procedures for resolving the problems illustrated by cases 1–4 (except, of course, the students' forms of English verbal expression, which psychologists assure us will improve with maturation) will be suggested. Finally, some common reactions to the suggestions proposed will be analyzed and, in conclusion, colleagues will be urged to be aware of choices that must be made.

Before considering guidelines for use of a textbook, advice on the nature and use of instructional materials generated by the profession must be looked at. Widely distributed curriculum guides and some other materials written by groups of recognized classroom teachers are good indicators of what leading authorities think ought to be considered as local curricula. A look at one such guide of nearly thirty years ago (Brisley et al., 2) will show us that we were once urged to consider language learning as a product of what the *teacher* does. But, a look at a guide of much more recent vintage indicates that we are also asked to consider what the *student* does (Strasheim and Bartz, 7). We are also asked to consider two products: language learning and language acquisition. That is, we are asked to consider both the learning of skills and the practicing of them (Rivers, 6). If we stop to think how we language teachers, as lifelong learners and acquirers of second language skills, continue to add to our own second language abilities, we can readily see the importance of providing for both. Here is an anonymous teacher's example:

Example A

I was in Argentina one summer and found myself in a conversation with a friend to whom I wanted to say something like "The grass is always greener on the other side." It would have been the perfect resolution to the situation we were discussing. I knew better than to try a word-for-word translation and settled for an alternative resolution. But my curiosity was piqued. I asked one bilingual friend after another. I was using the help of each of these friends as one might use a computerized data base. Finally, I came up with a hypothesis that I will hold until I find a better one: *La suerte de la fea, la linda la desea.*

What our anonymous colleague has told us here is that he added to his Spanish communicative ability because his own curiosity posed a problem he set out to solve. He acquired new linguistic competence by checking other sources of data (people, in this case). He did not study, as one might for a test, and he may (or may not) discover a better solution at some point. This kind of skill acquisition does not obviate ordinary point-to-point linear teaching and learning. A colleague illustrates that fact with a second example.

Example B

I knew that Argentines use an informal form of address not found in textbooks (*vos*). I wanted to learn to use it while there and asked a friend for help. I was told not to ruin perfectly good Spanish with slang. That was, I presume, a polite reason not to give me a grammar lesson that might have taught me the desired forms. A grammar book that might have taught them to me was not available. Asking my friends to help wasn't working either. So, I used written forms that appeared in novels, on greeting cards, and even on billboards (from which I learned some of the imperatives) to make my own grammar lesson and learn to use the *vos* form.

In this case, the anonymous colleague has shown that he learned the desired forms in a structured form—one that is most commonly found in classrooms and textbooks. Curriculum guides of recent vintage ask users to consider not only the teaching and learning in example B, but the acquisition illustrated in example A. Why? Because high school students and adults alike use both as they develop second language proficiency. One procedure develops a need for the other and they operate together in a reciprocal fashion.

Textbooks provide for learning (as in example B), but they tend to provide fewer opportunities for acquisition (as in example A). The future will probably see them provide more, but the best acquisition activity results from a problem posed by the student. Textbooks cannot respond flexibly to any problem a student may pose, but computers, of course, can use software like *Systeme D* to do exactly that (Noblitt et al., 4). With this view of the state of the professional art in mind, some guidelines for making the best possible use of the textbook are proposed.

Textbook Guidelines

The first step toward making efficient use of a textbook is to collect all the language-teaching material one has available. These will include textbooks and their visuals, workbooks, and other peripherals. The resulting array will be astounding and one will naturally have the feeling that using even a part of it along with a textbook will mean sacrificing some essential part of the year's work. It is natural and normal to feel the contrasting pressures of new and exciting ideas gathered from nontext sources against those of the textbook. Here are some questions likely to arise. Must one "cover" the text at any cost? Is it impossible to take advantage of fresh ideas without costing the students essential knowledge? Are the people who actually use the foreign language for communicative purposes ignoring important lessons about the nature of language that students need? The reader has probably answered all three questions negatively. Is it normal to feel some hesitation at doing so? Yes—perfectly normal. To answer the above three questions negatively implies that one is going to make some of one's own decisions about what will and will not be taught.

The second step toward successful textbook use is to make cuts in the array of material. The teacher who has not done a lot of this before, whether experienced or not, is going to feel uneasy. It is a situation akin to learning to drive. One's first times out are frightening whether one admits it or not. It is also necessary to find an alternative to the most common way to plan a semester of instruction.

Whether it is the "correct" way or not, the most common way to determine intended educational outcome is to peruse the textbook, divide and subdivide it, and thus produce a statement of "how many chapters per grading period will be covered." That is, while not many people will publicly say so, the usual procedure is to open the text to the table of contents and divide the number of chapters by the number of weeks in a semester. The most severe drawback of this procedure is that it precludes selectivity, turning over all the decision making to the design of the textbook while publishers and authors alike tend to deliberately overwrite their materials with an eye toward encouraging selectivity. To make selectivity possible, one begins with an array of texts, not just the one adopted. At that point, it is clearly impossible to teach and learn everything that lies before one's eyes. It makes sense to select some functions students will be able to perform in the target language. These are frequently indicated in recent curriculum guides and Omaggio (5) lists 190 such functions in Appendix B of her book. One could also survey students to find out about functional goals they might suggest. Because learning and acquisition can comfortably coexist, one may be especially interested in selecting functions that can be tied to a grammatical goal. For example, to deny an allegation (a perfectly valid functional goal) one is likely to need the subjunctive in Spanish (a well-known grammatical goal). There is no reason the grammatical goal cannot underlie the functional one, but it is important to deemphasize some grammatical goals tied to functional ones that have not been chosen.

Other candidates for deemphasis may include items that do not appear in every book examined. The resulting cuts will leave time and space for locally selected items that have special appeal to students and teachers alike (perhaps songs, proverbs, simulations, dramas, communicative devices, listening exercises, readings, and a host of other things to be seen at any foreign language conference). Teachers will be the first to recognize that it takes courage to make the deemphases we speak of. They will necessarily face dissension, but that can be constructive—especially if it is made clear that the deemphases proposed are being proposed only for the coming year, not for permanent preservation in stone. Curriculum is supposed to be cyclical in nature. One does not make a curriculum plan without an eye to improving it for subsequent use. So, each year in each language, teachers must decide on the minimum that each teacher can safely demand of any and all students. It must be agreed that each teacher will add to the minimum as he or she sees fit. It must also be agreed that no more than the minimum will be expected at subsequent levels. Then, each teacher can supplement the minimum as needed.

The ESL field is well known to be methodologically sophisticated. It often seems that ESL students and teachers leave their foreign language colleagues far behind. ESL classes tend not to have large-scale comprehensive textbooks. Instead, they tend to have readers and a host of supplementary materials. Perhaps the success of our ESL colleagues should be examined with greater care as we make the third step of this procedure: recombining to build a curriculum.

As noted above, it is critical to reach consensus. As one builds the new curriculum, having examined an array of materials and having established deemphases of the least essential aspects of the comprehensive text, one seeks consensus by being carefully diplomatic. Once basic items have been selected, it must be agreed that those basic items, in combination with items that each teacher selects independently, constitute mastery of the level at hand. This precludes one from indicating that colleagues whose work has been different have been remiss. If their students master the minimum plus teacher-selected supplements, they must be seen as having mastered the level under discussion, albeit, perhaps, in a different way. To continue reassembly, one must make a statement of what students are to accomplish in the course. This is the trip that the textbook (or road map) can help us take. It is fortunate that it is easier for foreign language teachers to make clear statements of expected behavioral outcomes of teaching than it is for many other teachers. Our basic goals are always listening, speaking, reading, writing, and arriving at some level of appreciation of a different culture. This appears to restate the obvious until we see that it means that teachers must agree on a minimal level. Since there is a strong tendency to resist such agreement, the step we now propose becomes more of a real achievement.

Having established a selected minimal competency standard (that is, a group of functional goals and underlying grammatical goals plus some goals selected by the individual teacher) for a particular level, a local curriculum committee then needs to work together to establish a curriculum at the departmental level. This may entail a communicative process among several professionals that teachers simply aren't used to. It is a process that demands an open attitude about what one can truly accomplish and forbids criticism and negative feedback. A comment like "If you keep watering down the curriculum with inanities like that, none of us will have jobs" does no good for anyone. But if one feels a need to state goals in more rigorous terms, something like "I have a different set of needs" gets the need expressed without disparaging others. We suggest that teachers will need to develop communicative patterns that are different from those one sometimes observes in workrooms. Here are some basic rules.

Developing Communicative Patterns

1. *Communicating is more important than winning.* The end product is to last a maximum of one year and can even be changed in less time if the need is pressing enough. The goodwill and enthusiasm generated by focusing on the communication outweighs the short-lived joy of "winning" a dispute. The surest road to paralysis is "I (You) can't do that."

2. *Brainstorming implies freedom from negative feedback.* When attempting to find mutually acceptable ways to establish and implement local proficiency standards, it is best to make a record of every suggestion and statement. Spend more time making statements of what might be done and none at all on delineating the negative features of ideas presented.

3. *Don't sermonize.* People who are always shown the error of their ways will not contribute to the discussion. Communication will be impaired if much value is attached to finding the correct way before all the various alternatives are at least given a hearing.

4. *Be open to the message of our elementary school colleagues.* The nature of secondary schools leads foreign language teachers to emphasize the teaching of a given subject at the cost of an emphasis on the development of the children we teach. Glib lines like "High school teachers teach subjects, while elementary teachers teach kids" describe the problem without solving it. The solution lies in recognizing that foreign language teachers are more elementary in their outlook than some of their colleagues. They must be that way to succeed because foreign language classes begin at the beginning, with sound and symbol and their relationships. They must teach one concept at a time, move from known items to the unknown, and emphasize the concrete. These principles are vital to success in foreign language curriculum building.

5. *Emphasize active learning and peer interaction.* In a curriculum that is organized around function, grammatical content is encountered when, if, and as needed to accomplish the function at hand. Students need to use and apply the structures they are learning. They need to acquire as well as learn because concepts are readily internalized if one experiences the language by seeing, saying, and

doing. Also, processes that are student-centered (such as peer correction of writing, etc.) get high praise in evaluations of teaching. Remarks like "We learn most from each other in groups" are not surprising. Peer learning is a good way to build in the skill-using that can lead to real classroom acquisition of a foreign language. It also relieves fear of being embarrassed over perfectly normal errors.

The Outcome

Now, let us consider the question of finding out how well the combination of skill-getting and skill-using can work. There are two kinds of evaluations that will help examine the value of active participation in local curriculum design. The first is process-oriented. To accomplish it, one need only measure such things as enrollment trends and participation by students and teachers alike. The second is product-oriented. To measure product, one might look at retention figures, teacher satisfaction, and student achievement. There may also be something to be said for using the nationally established proficiency guidelines to do this, but it is not absolutely essential to start with them. After all, revamping objectives and rethinking the way one uses resources like textbooks are big enough orders for one semester's work. It may be advisable to do one thing at a time.

In a sense, a gauntlet has been thrown down here. The teacher is left with the challenge to communicate with colleagues or not. The recent Carnegie Foundation for the Advancement of Teaching study notes that teachers have relatively little to say about making critical decisions. Textbook selection and implementation, however, are areas where teachers do have significant power (Boyer, 1).

There is more than one system of classroom management wherein the student is directed to face choices he or she must make in order to maintain the learning process. Perhaps it can be said that, in this case, we need to give our colleagues direct information about the problems illustrated by cases 1–4 earlier in this article. They are real enough and they stem from our pattern of trying to use every page of our textbooks. Our tendency is to use textbooks as if they were antibiotics prescribed by our doctors. ("Take all this medicine even if you feel better before finishing it.") The reason for this tendency is not clear, but a survey reported by

W. D. McInerney of Purdue University (3) indicates that the cover-the-textbook syndrome is caused by internal pressures that teachers believe are imposed externally. The responsibility of teachers is to communicate with colleagues and design local curriculum with the textbook as a guide rather than as a list of things to do. There is no need to divorce oneself from the textbook, but an arm's length of separation seems well worth the time needed to effect it.

References

1. Boyer, Ernest L. *Teacher Involvement in Decisionmaking: A State by State Profile*. Princeton, NJ: Carnegie Foundation for the Advancement of Teaching, 1988.
2. Brisley, Leonard, et al. *Good Teaching Practices: A Survey of High School Foreign Language Classes*. New York: Modern Language Association of America, 1961 (ERIC ED 003 946).
3. McInerney, W. D. "Establishing University–School District Collaboration in the Education of Teachers." Unpublished paper presented at American Educational Research Association Conference, Washington, DC, 1987.
4. Noblitt, James S., et al. *Systeme D*. Boston: Heinle and Heinle, 1988.
5. Omaggio, Alice C. *Teaching Language in Context: Proficiency-Oriented Instruction*. Boston: Heinle and Heinle, 1986.
6. Rivers, Wilga M. *Speaking in Many Tongues: Essays in Foreign-Language Teaching*. Third Edition. New York: Cambridge University Press, 1983.
7. Strasheim, Lorraine A., and Walter H. Bartz, eds. *A Guide to Proficiency-Based Instruction in Modern Foreign Languages in Indiana Schools*. Indianapolis: Center for School Improvement and Performance, Department of Education, 1986.

8
The Past Meets the Present: A Guide to Historical Feature Films in the French Culture Class

Tom Carr
University of Nebraska–Lincoln

The numerous feature films dealing with the French Revolution such as *Danton*[1] or Jean Renoir's *La Marseillaise*[2] make the Bicentenary in 1989 an appropriate moment for reviewing how movies dealing with the past can add historical perspective to our civilization classes. Too often we concentrate attention almost exclusively on contemporary culture. Our neglect of the past, however, is seldom due to disinterest. We lack approaches for developing student interest in the past that has, in large measure, shaped the patterns of life today.

Feature films offer a vehicle for catching students up in history and they allow students to visualize how people lived in previous eras, fleshing out the names of historical figures that might otherwise remain abstract and, at the same time, allowing students to witness momentous events.

This gripping immediacy that film lends to whatever it depicts, however, makes instructors rightly wary of using movies for teaching about the past. Feature films are not documentaries, and they may impart more misconceptions than accurate information. Films allow us to visualize only a past reconstructed by a director. Even if the filmmaker takes every precaution to make his reconstitution as authentic as possible, using the most accurate information historians of the day can provide, as in the case of *Le Retour de Martin Guerre*, the movie is still nothing more than an imaginative re-creation. Even more troubling, the quest for a gripping plot, or spectacle, or for vivid characters, may lead the director to sacrifice authenticity for fictional excitement. Commercial feature films are, above all, intended as entertainment.

Feature films with a historical subject are indeed documents, but more often than not they tell us more about the values and mores of the era in which they were produced than of the periods they purport to portray. In the most rigorous sense, *La Marseillaise* documents more directly what the French public in 1938 thought of the events of 1792 than the actual attitude of the revolutionary troops or the royal family in 1792. As a reconstitution of the storming of the Tuileries, the film may be more or less faithful to history; it reflects most accurately the clichés, stereotypes, and interpretations of the Revolution current in the last days of the Popular Front.

Nonetheless, although trial records from the revolutionary tribunal in 1794 might be the most appropriate documents in a history class focusing on the Reign of Terror, a film such as *Danton* is ideal in a culture course. Our civilization classes cannot afford to treat either the past or the present in splendid isolation; each must be presented with due regard for the other. Culture classes whose primary focus is contemporary civilization cannot ignore the way in which the past shapes current reality, often in ways today's generations are not aware, thus the need to explore even the aspects of the past that do not seem immediately relevant. Likewise, even when focusing primarily on history, culture classes must take into account how the past lives on in the consciousness of present generations, not so much in the research of professional historians as in symbols, stereotypes, and legend. Indeed, feature films are one of the most powerful ways in which such myths become fixed in the popular imagination.

We owe it to our students to acquaint them with the perceptions that members of the target culture share about their past, but we also should provide the tools for a critical assessment of such myths by making use of the resources provided by historians. The suggestions here go beyond enjoying the imaginative appeal of feature films to examine how they can be used to study both the period they portray and the one in which they were made. In honor of the Bicentenary, these illustrations are taken from films treating the Revolution that are available on videocassette in the United States,[3] but the model and suggestions apply to any historical period (for example, France's experience in World War II), or to any country for that matter.

Selecting Points to Emphasize

Even though a class rarely has time to undertake a comprehensive analysis of a film, the instructor should have in mind the range of possibilities in order to select the most pertinent elements for study. Figure 1 shows how the image of the past portrayed in the movie can be shaped by two sometimes competing impulses—the desire to impose an interpretation on history, and the need to present the past in an entertaining way. Interpretation and entertainment represent the forces of the present that mold the way the various aspects of the past are portrayed in the movie.

Figure 1

PORTRAIT OF THE PAST

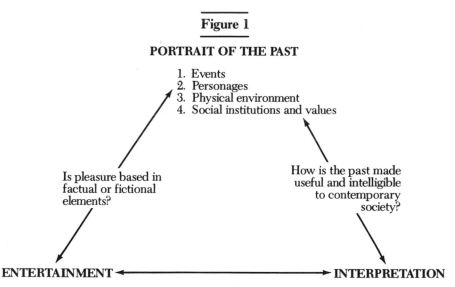

1. Events
2. Personages
3. Physical environment
4. Social institutions and values

Is pleasure based in factual or fictional elements?

How is the past made useful and intelligible to contemporary society?

ENTERTAINMENT ◄————————————► **INTERPRETATION**

Does the desire to please blunt or sensationalize the thesis?

For purposes of convenience, four such aspects can be distinguished. In each case we find a spectrum of authenticity running from efforts that are completely fictional to those that anchor the portrait faithfully in historical models.

A film can highlight (1) *historical events,* whether as vignettes such as Marat's murder in *Napoléon,*[4] or as a panoramic account such as the fall of the monarchy in the summer of 1792 that comprises the action of *La Marseillaise*. The events of the plot can be almost completely fictionalized but set against a background of allusions to historical facts, as in *Les Mariés de l'An II*,[5] or they can give the appearance of a meticulous reconstitution, as in *Danton*.

The (2) *historical personages* who enact the events constitute the second element. In *La Nuit de Varennes*,[6] the royal family's flight from Paris in 1791 is little more than a pretext for the invented encounter of a mixture of figures with authentic models like Tom Paine and Casanova and fictional ones who are nonetheless representative of The Ancien Régime. *La Marseillaise* contrasts the real members of the royal court with fictional soldiers representing a cross section of the Revolution; the anonymous soldiers from the Midi who are given names and substance for the duration of the film succeed in overthrowing Louis XVI and his queen. *Danton*, on the other hand, is populated almost entirely with characters modeled on history, while in *Les Mariés*, except for references to a few historical figures, the cast of characters is drawn from historical romances.

Two aspects forming the background are sometimes as interesting as the events and characters that occupy center stage: (3) *the physical setting* including buildings, furniture, clothes, food, and the like, and (4) *the social roles and institutions and value systems* within which the characters act. Women's role in the Revolution might be compared in *Napoléon* and *La Marseillaise;* the aristocratic ethos of the courtiers in *La Marseillaise* might be contrasted with the depiction of the outlook of the lower classes. Revolutionary justice could be studied in terms of the functioning of the tribunal in *Danton*. Allusions to new foodstuffs like tomatoes in *La Marseillaise* are examples of how the texture of daily life can be highlighted.

As rich as such a portrait of life in past eras may be, it cannot be taken at face value. In a sense, no matter how much the filmmakers strive for authenticity, their creations remain essentially works of fiction. Danton is Gérard Depardieu; Louis XVI is Jean Renoir's brother Pierre. Even when the original sites are used, as the Luxembourg Palace where the Dantonists were imprisoned, the site has been restored and sanitized according to twentieth century norms. The past we witness in feature films has been transformed for consumption by present-day audiences. However, rather than lament this fact, we should exploit it in our civilization classes by examining the interplay between history and contemporary attitudes.

The Portrait of the Past: Accuracy and Clichés

1. Assessing Accuracy.   Two tasks are really involved here: *describing* the aspects selected for study and then *comparing* them to more complete sources of information.

First, students might pretend they are anthropologists or historians studying some alien culture with professional detachment. They will quickly discover that while an anthropologist is able to observe the complete way of life of the subjects, they can only note those subjects that have been selected for inclusion by the filmmaker. Furthermore, within this limited selection, certain points have been emphasized in the movie. The same selective procedure will be found at work in the presentation of events or the biographies of historical figures.

The second step is to assess this description for accuracy. It might be compared with original documents dating from the period, such as speeches from Danton's trial or Napoléon's memoirs, or with historians' accounts, whether in textbooks or reference materials. Instructors must consider accessibility of library resources and their students' ability in assigning such work. Given what is known today about the period under consideration, what items have been omitted, invented, or distorted? In later sections we will see to what extent such omissions or distortions are due to the desire to entertain or present a thesis.

2. Identifying Clichés.   While assessing accuracy transforms students into historians evaluating how faithful the film is to the past, examining a movie's clichés is an implicit acknowledgment that popular audiences are less concerned with what the past might really have been like than with what they *believe* the past was like. For them history is more a tissue of images, slogans, and myths acquired from television, history textbooks, or patriotic celebrations than a tidy chronology of precise facts. These clichés belong to informal culture rather than to the formal world of scholarship, and thus students cannot find them conveniently cataloged in reference books. They must be pointed out by the instructor, who might refer students to other occurrences in popular culture or art. A few examples of clichés in American films can familiarize students with the concept of these images that generate an automatic response in audiences sharing the same cultural background.

Such widely shared notions implant themselves easily in the popular consciousness because they are *simplifications* with *an attached emotional charge*. Students might want to use their historical research to analyze how clichés simplify the past, just as their work with contemporary culture can lead them to examine the emotional bond that clichés establish between the present and the past.

Even when such widely held notions are not analyzed by students, they will come away from the film with an exposure to the same powerful vehicle for communicating such clichés that members of the target culture themselves experience. *Les Mariés* is a storehouse of such clichés, which serve as local color for an adventure story that might have taken place anywhere.

Interpretation: The Intelligible Past and the Useful Past

The selective memory that accounts for the incomplete nature of the film's portrait of the past is, in great measure, a function of the filmmaker's attempt to make the past meaningful. In part, this meaning results from the patterns of explanation used to render intelligible the often chaotic events of the past; in part, it derives from making the past serve present-day concerns. The first emphasizes the order that historians impose on past events; the second deals with the many ways in which history is put to use in contemporary society.

1. Patterns of Intelligibility.   In addition to chronology, the *forms of causality* invoked provide the most common method for imparting coherence. Thus, while the opening scenes of *Danton* briefly allude to the social problems caused by the war to defend the Revolution (rationing, conscription, etc.), the Revolution itself is seen as the clash of two vigorous personalities. With more than a touch of hubris, Danton has utter confidence in the power of his charisma over the people, while Robespierre sees himself with false modesty as the interpreter of the popular revolutionary will. On the other hand, *La Marseillaise* stresses the grievances of the lower classes as a cause of the Revolution and shows events as the product of impersonal collective forces rather than of dominant individuals.

Moreover, such forms of causality often are a function of a larger thesis the film presents in its attempt to interpret history. *Danton* argues against sacrificing justice to political expediency; *La Marseillaise* shows the Revolution as the triumph of the productive classes over an ineffective aristocracy.

When such a thesis can be identified, students can ask whether it was standard in the period when the film was made. For example, *Danton*, filmed in 1982, denounced political terror exercised by a small group in the name of the revolutionary masses just when Marxism's appeal to the French intelligentsia was waning. In addition, discussing how plot, characterization, and visual effects reinforce the thesis is also rewarding.

2. Using the Past.   Such interpretations are seldom merely scholarly disputes among historians, but are motivated by the desire to appropriate the past for the needs of current generations. Thus the film must be situated in terms of the social trends and economic conditions of the period when it was released. Renoir was a fellow traveler during the Popular Front, and while his film is no crude propaganda piece, it does echo many themes promoted by the Party during this period. The Polish director Andrzei Wajda establishes parallels in *Danton* between the revolutionary tribunal and the Stalinist show trials in Eastern Europe. Indeed, films often highlight some situation in the past, not so much in terms of its significance then, but because of *the parallels audiences will automatically establish with some social problem in contemporary society*. This is one of the most fruitful areas for study because it allows students to compare the same issue in two very different sets of circumstances.

Some films become political events in themselves that mobilize public opinion. However, this quest for social relevance is far from the only use the present makes of history. Many feature films set in the past exploit an escapist nostalgia, for a lost golden age, for example. Others settle for patriotic identification with national heroes in which audiences forget their present divisions and share communion in a common past that unites them. *Les Mariés,* which alludes to the touchy issue of the Chouans' Catholicism, shows the French united in the last scenes against a foreign enemy.

Students can gain some objective measure of the film's effect if they study the movie's reception by examining reviews or box office statistics.

Entertainment: The Pleasures of the Past

Many liberties a film takes with historical accuracy can be traced to the need to entertain. If the movie is to be a commercial success, it cannot risk offending the values and received notions of its intended audience. Familiar clichés may be more appealing than stark authenticity, and a controversial thesis may alienate a large number of viewers. Thus, *La Marseillaise* takes care to include patriotic royalists and ends with a note of nationalistic fervor on the eve of the great victory of Valmy. Conversely, since movie audiences today have a great appetite for bloody violence, *Danton* shows its hero's execution in gory detail that might not have been possible in an earlier era.

In addition, it is helpful to examine the extent to which the depiction of the past is the source of entertainment by studying the mixture of historical and fictional elements in the film. Is the film gripping because of the historical events it portrays or because of elements that have been invented? While history records the events of the past with considerable precision, the personal motivations that drive men and women to act must often be inferred. This human factor of psychological drama that audiences find so absorbing must be invented in most cases with varying degrees of plausibility.

Do the fictional elements reinforce and complement the historical ones or detract from them? How is the obligatory love interest handled: Is it subordinate to the political action as in *Danton* or does it constitute the chief source of motivation as in *Les Mariés*? To what extent does the use of stars like Belmondo or Depardieu influence the way the audience perceives the characters they portray?

Getting Started

The sole ironclad rules are never to show a film without first previewing it for suitability and without having a clear notion of pedagogical goals. Other potential problems should also be addressed with attention to advantages and disadvantages of possible solutions.

Should the films be shown in segments or as a whole? Since most films are too long for a single class period, showing them in several episodes is often unavoidable. This can allow the instructor to present a focused introduction to the aspects of the segment to be highlighted, and allow for adequate followup while the scene is still fresh in students' minds. Just the same, students should have the opportunity to catch the whole sweep of the film by seeing it in a single sitting, either before or after it is broken down into segments. Just as one would hesitate to analyze a novel based on a single reading, film study should rely on multiple viewings. Ideally, students should have access to the cassette to verify hypotheses and recollections.

While it is crucial to compare the film to more reliable sources of information, just when and how they should be introduced depends on many factors. Showing a film to unprepared students can blunt its entertainment value as well as its pedagogical interest. Films often assume familiarity by the audience with allusions to a cultural context that can leave outsiders like our students baffled. Moreover, alerting students ahead of time to inaccuracies can lessen the chance that they will absorb these inaccuracies uncritically. A film shown at the end of a unit can serve to synthesize a particular period, or it can be introduced early on with only minimal initial preparation as motivation for students to undertake further research.

For best results students should be given a viewing guide listing characters, pertinent vocabulary, and information about the film's production (Carr and Duncan, 1). When assessing the extent to which a film reflects a particular period's interpretation of history, it is important to ascertain which version of the film the students are watching (Sorlin, 6). Films are frequently edited for re-release (or for packaging as cassettes), and it is not always safe to assume that the version at hand corresponds to the date when the movie was shot. For example, Abel Gance's *Napoléon* has been edited and "restored" many times since its first release in 1927; the Francis Ford Coppola presentation available on cassette eliminates the scenes showing the violent infatuation of Joséphine's maid Violine for the Corsican general.

The viewing guide can also be used to prepare students for a fruitful postviewing discussion by indicating the elements of the film that the instructor wishes to highlight.

When several films dealing with the same subject are available, excerpts from films that the instructor does not wish to show in their entirety can be compared to the one selected for intensive study. Rouget de Lisle's anthem appears in *Napoléon* and *Danton* as well as in *La Marseillaise*. Both *La Nuit de Varennes* and *La Marseillaise* contain puppet shows enacting the conflict between the monarchy and the people. Robespierre directs the Reign of Terror in *Danton* and *Napoléon*. Showing a clip from a movie that presents much the same scene but with a different style or interpretation can remind students that no matter how realistic movies seem, they are constructed out of arbitrary cinematographic conventions. Thanks to the immediacy of film, the same event can be presented with contradictory, but equally plausible, interpretations in different movies.

Finally, leave room to pursue the spontaneous reactions of students. It is difficult to predict just which features of a movie will intrigue them, but their queries and comments can be followed up with profit.

Activities for Lower-Level Classes

If discussion is to be limited to the target language, students must be supplied vocabulary and information by the instructor. Rather than rely on the students to do research, the instructor should provide the essential data needed to interpret the film.

1. Prepare a list of quotations in the order they appear in the film. This provides vocabulary in context for students who can be asked to identify the character speaking and to describe the situation.

2. True/false statements describing the action and characters in the order found in the film can incorporate additional vocabulary. Students work through them as they watch the movie. By including controversial interpretations or judgments about the film, the T/F activities facilitate focused discussion as students correct false statements and illustrate the ones with which they agree.

3. Cultural spinoffs give students an opportunity to experience more fully the cultural icons to which the film alludes. *La Marseillaise* is a revolutionary songfest giving students an opportunity to sing *Ça ira, La Carmagnole, La Marseillaise,* and even other less familiar songs such as Gretry's *Richard o mon roi.*

   Likewise, allusions to celebrated artworks such as David's *La Mort de Marat* in *Napoléon,* or to his *Serment du Jeu de Paume* in *Danton* can be pursued. Famous sites can be discussed. The Luxembourg Palace built for Marie de Médicis in the sixteenth century housed political prisoners like Danton during the Revolution before becoming the seat of today's French Senate.

4. "Back from the dead" allows some figure from the era depicted in the film to review it for accuracy. "Real" historical personages can also react to their portrayal in the movie.

5. Select a few key scenes for intense critical analysis after students have seen the entire film.

Conclusion

Since the past meets the present in historical feature films, they offer a unique document for culture classes. Success in exploiting their potential depends on having a grasp of how such films simultaneously both depict historical events and reflect contemporary concerns. This paper has suggested a range of broad approaches for dealing with films as they portray and interpret the past and make it entertaining, as well as a number of specific strategies for implementing them. The principles behind these approaches should help instructors develop further strategies adapted to their own circumstances.

Notes

1. *Danton* (1982)   This Franco-Polish co-production assumes that the viewer is familiar with the events leading up to the Reign of Terror, but is gripping nonetheless as two powerful personalities, Danton and Robespierre, clash, each with his own attitude toward the use of violence in politics. Its drawback is graphic depiction of Danton's execution.
2. *La Marseillaise* (1937)   Jean Renoir's account of the participation of a group of soldiers from Marseilles in the fall of the monarchy in 1792 portrays the attitudes of all classes of society to the Revolution. Drawbacks are that the film is in black and white and contains meridional accents.
3. The following firms carry some or all of these films: Polyglot Productions, Box 668, Cambridge, MA 02238-0668; Facets Multimedia, 1517 W. Fullerton Avenue, Chicago, IL 60614; Tamarelle's International Films, 110 Cohasset Stage Rd., Chico, CA 95926.
4. *Napoléon* (1927)   Although Napoléon was not a major actor in the first five years of the Revolution, Gance's film includes many episodes depicted in other films. Drawbacks of the film include the fact that it is silent, is four hours in length, and has captions in English.
5. *Les Mariés de l'An II*   An action film with Jean-Paul Belmondo set during the Vendée counterrevolution, it is interesting for its reliance on clichés.
6. *La Nuit de Varennes* (1982)   The royal family's attempt to flee Paris in 1791 is pretext for stimulating discussions between such real eighteenth century figures as Casanova, Rétif de la Bretonne, and Tom Paine. Its drawback is very little action and much talk.

References

1. Carr, Tom, and Jan Duncan. "The VCR Revolution: Feature Films for Language and Cultural Proficiency," in Diane W. Birckbichler, ed., *Proficiency, Policy, and Professionalism in Foreign Language Education,* Report of the Central States Conference on the Teaching of Foreign Languages. Lincolnwood, IL: National Textbook Company, 1987.
2. Ferro, Marc. "Does a Filmic Writing of History Exist?" *Film and History* 17 (1987):81–89.
3. Garrity, Henry. *Film in the French Classroom.* Cambridge, MA: Polyglot Productions, 1987.
4. Murray, Lawrence L. *The Celluloid Persuasion: Movies and the Liberal Arts.* Grand Rapids, MI: William B. Eerdmans, 1979.
5. Smith, Paul, ed. *The Historian and Film.* Cambridge, MA: Cambridge University Press, 1976.
6. Sorlin, Pierre. *The Film in History: Restaging the Past.* Totowa, NJ: Barnes and Noble, 1980.

9
Crossing the Rubicon: Bridging the Gap between "Grammar" and "Literature" in the Intermediate Latin Course

Jeffrey L. Buller
Loras College, Dubuque, Iowa

Not long ago, in the Good Old Days—or the Bad Old Days, depending upon your perspective—there was one line of Latin that nearly everyone knew by heart:

> *Gallia est omnis divisa in partes tres.*
> "All Gaul has been divided into three parts."

This quotation comes, of course, from the opening to Caesar's *Gallic Wars*. And, in an age when students who wished to go to college were urged, and sometimes compelled, to take Latin, this line was as famous as any in literature. Later in life, few of those who remembered these words might recall why the land of Gaul had attained this unusual distinction, and even fewer could be expected to name what the three parts were. But none of that seemed as important as the line itself; it was a quotation that tended to remain memorable long after the rest of Caesar's campaigns, and his ablatives absolute, were nothing more than a distant memory.

The reason the opening to the *Gallic Wars* remained so memorable was that it was the first line of real Latin that most students had ever seen.

Generations of scholars learned their Latin by studying sentences that illustrated sound grammatical principles, but that contained little sense and less interest. After months of reading about farmers who carried roses into the forest and sailors or poets who lived on a small island, the *Gallic Wars* must have come as something of a relief. This work provided a bridge from the study of Latin as grammar to the reading of Latin as literature. Exposure to Caesar was thus an important rite of passage: all of those deponents and supines, so painfully mastered, could finally be used for something. And, best of all, Caesar's opening words actually seemed to make sense.

Students, therefore, were able to read and understand an original work by a major author after only a single year of Latin. But that pleasure is now being shared by surprisingly few of their successors. It is not that Latin is unpopular today. As teachers across the country will readily attest, enrollments in Latin have, within the past ten years, risen dramatically. Schools that once eliminated or reduced their Latin programs are often reinstating or expanding them. So overwhelming, in fact, is this resurgence of Latin that there has been a severe shortage of Latin teachers in several states.

Criticism against Using Caesar's *Gallic Wars*

Unfortunately, what has been good for Latin has not necessarily been good for Caesar. That old quadrivium known as the "standard Latin curriculum"—four years of "grammar, Caesar, Cicero, and Vergil," once as invariable as *fero, ferre, tuli, latum*—has, in recent years, come under increasing fire. Caesar, it seems, is no longer fashionable. But, what is worse, he is regarded as somehow unsuitable for the modern curriculum. To be precise, three charges are now being heard against Caesar, even among Latin teachers themselves:

1. That Caesar, as a figure who frequently used military force to solve political problems, has no place in the modern curriculum. Two world wars, and innumerable other conflicts, have exposed the folly of rampant militarism. Increasingly, courses today, even at the high school level, are devoted to teaching students about the necessity of peace. As a result, the works of Caesar, in which we see brute force so often triumphant, are no longer appropriate for

high school students. The youth of today would find the world depicted in the *Gallic Wars* to be dated at best and dangerous at worst.

2. That students frequently enter high school with far less background in "traditional grammar" than was once the case; as a result, completing an introductory Latin text now requires nearly two full years. More time must be spent, it is said, in explaining to students the nature and use of such fundamental points of grammar as nouns, verbs, participles, infinitives, and cases. To compensate for the additional time needed for lessons in grammar, something had to be cut from the curriculum. Caesar, as the Latin author whom students and teachers alike have often found "least interesting," was the logical choice.

3. That the lack of uniformity in modern curricula does not provide students with sufficient background to understand Caesar. At one time, many argue, students read the *Gallic Wars* soon after studying Shakespeare's *Julius Caesar* in their English classes and the First Triumvirate and Roman Civil Wars in their world history classes. But there is far greater diversity in the courses offered at high schools today. Most students, therefore, will lack the historical knowledge needed to understand Caesar's text.

These arguments are taking their toll. Caesar's place in the "standard Latin curriculum" is increasingly being filled with stories about Hercules and Perseus, adaptations of or selections from other authors, additional lessons on Latin grammar—or with nothing at all. This is not an exaggeration. Several series, most notably *Ecce Romani* (24), give Caesar barely a nod and go directly to Cicero. "Do not pass Gaul. Do not collect 200 deponents."

Rationale for Including the *Gallic Wars* in Today's Curriculum

This situation is all the more regrettable because that once familiar bridge between grammar and literature is no longer being crossed. The *Gallic Wars* was important precisely because it guided students from the artificial world of syntactical exercises to the "real world" of literature. Caesar's Rome was one in which both his politics and his grammar were marked by their irregularities, their obscurities—and their memorable phrases. In Caesar, students found an author who was (1) understandable without being adapted beyond all recognition, (2) important as a pivotal figure in western history, and (3) stylistically identifiable from first word to last. That is an impressive list of qualities for an author who can be read so early in the study of a language.

The recent criticism of Caesar, therefore, must not be permitted to go unchallenged. For, as to the first objection, it should be noted that no one can proclaim the merits of peace simply by ignoring acts of war. To be sure, in a study of peace, authors like Caesar increase their value because they reveal the causes of human conflict. In a course on Caesar, students will frequently discuss such issues as whether the Gallic campaigns were justified in the first place, whether Caesar's reputation for "clemency" was earned, and whether the breach with Pompey was truly inevitable. Teachers of Latin have always insisted that the ancient world still has lessons for today. In light of this belief, they, above all, should understand that Caesar's text introduces students to a struggle as vivid as any of those in modern times. And the lessons to be learned from such conflicts will be lost if we fail to study the authors who describe them.

Secondly, far from interfering with the lessons in grammar that many students need, Caesar can actually provide a useful source for these lessons. From the very beginning of the *Gallic Wars*, students will encounter a text that is not particularly difficult. Caesar's sentences tend to be short, his vocabulary easy, his style unadorned. As a result of these qualities, the teacher of Latin can use the *Gallic Wars* to build upon the foundations of grammar that have been laid in the first-year course. If such material as the sequence of tenses, the formation of indirect questions, and the passive periphrastic is no longer covered in first-year Latin, these structures may still be explained, as they occur, during the unit on Caesar. Indeed, these lessons tend to be more memorable for students because they involve grammatical principles seen in actual use, not in artificial exercises. Moreover, the *Gallic Wars* offers frequent opportunities for a class to discuss Roman history, culture, and literary style, matters that provide a welcome complement to the study of grammar itself.

Finally, if students are no longer encountering Caesar and the First Triumvirate in their English and history classes, this is all the more reason for including this material in a Latin course. Roman history is important, after all, not only because the Romans are our spiritual forebears, but also because their deeds have entered out intellectual life. The founders of our own country were familiar with the classics, and their view of such figures as Caesar, Catiline, and Sulla had an impact upon our form of government. As a result, we simply cannot understand the customs and constitution of our own state, much less those of other modern peoples, unless we have read the classics. This is why the Latin teacher, far from replacing Caesar in the intermediate course, should insist that all students be exposed to the *Gallic Wars*.

It is not enough, however, to say that Caesar still deserves to be taught. We need to understand how the *Gallic Wars* should be taught by instructors who have, in all sincerity, questioned the value of this work. We need, furthermore, to examine the ways in which Caesar's campaigns, with all their fury and bloodshed, can be reconciled with a curriculum in which violence is no longer celebrated and dictators no longer admired.

Rationale for the Traditional Role of Caesar in the Curriculum

Teachers who are assigned a course in Caesar should begin their preparation by asking this question: Why was Caesar included in the "standard Latin curriculum" in the first place? In all likelihood, most teachers would reply by saying that "Caesar is the first author read because he is the easiest Roman author that there is." This answer, however, though widely believed, is simply not correct. There are plenty of Latin authors who, in whole or in part, are at least as easy as Caesar. Aulus Gellius, Phaedrus, Cornelius Nepos, Saint Jerome, several poems by Catullus, whole passages of Livy and Ovid, Martial, the Carmina Burana, and parts of Plautus can all be read by the intermediate Latin student without any difficulty at all. Not surprisingly, these are the very authors whom many teachers have adopted to fill the place once occupied by Caesar.

Yet not one of these authors serves the purpose that caused Caesar to be included in the curriculum to begin with. The attraction of Caesar was not that he was easy, but that his style was simple. These two terms are not synonymous. Things are easy because of what we do; things are simple because of what they are. The more we develop a skill, for instance, the easier the use of that skill becomes. But, try as we like, we cannot change the simplicity of an object one iota. As an illustration, even the longest and most convoluted sentence ever written could still be called "easy" if it contained grammar, vocabulary, and a word order thoroughly familiar to whoever was reading it. But that sentence could never be called "simple." For, no matter how proficient our reading skills became, the sentence itself would still involve periods of substantial length. It would contain metaphors, similes, and other literary devices. It would resound with assonance, consonance, and the rhythmic balance of its coda. It would, in short, impress us with its majesty and not with its brevity. But brevity, in addition to such qualities as clarity and order, is essential to what we mean when we speak of the "simple style." And that brevity, clarity, and order are the hallmarks of the *Gallic Wars*.

Simplicity of Style in the *Gallic Wars*

Caesar, in other words, was admired because he represented many features of the Attic prose style ("using the speech of every day, though in a form refined by careful choice of words, and avoidance of all extravagance and over-elaborateness of phraseology" [Rose, 22, p. 162])[1] or, more correctly, the plain style of composition ("the most current idiom of standard speech...brought down to the most ordinary speech of every day").[2] As a literary model, Caesar represented one important style of writing; Cicero, with his longer periods, richer vocabulary, and more complex argumentation, represented another style.

Caesar and Cicero were incorporated into the "standard Latin curriculum" so that they would be encountered, at least in American high schools, in a student's sophomore and junior years respectively. This order was important. The students needed to master the simplicity of Caesar before going on to the complexity of Cicero. Moreover, the *Gallic Wars* would be read at a time when the students were just beginning to develop their own prose styles. The clarity and simplicity of Caesar's work could thus be used to provide an attractive model. Imitation of Caesar's syntax would help students to avoid reproducing in English the ornate subordination and absolute structures that they had studied during their first year of Latin. To further this end, exercises in prose composition, usually based upon Caesar, were often introduced as well. The *Gallic Wars* was thus valued for its phraseology at least as much as for the information it contained.

The *Gallic Wars* as a Model for Student Compositions

A survey of textbooks from the late nineteenth and early twentieth centuries tends to confirm this impression. For instance, Francis Ritchie, most famous nowadays for his *Fabulae Faciles* (21),[3] also wrote a textbook in Latin prose composition based upon Caesar (20).[4] This work, first published in 1893, was regularly revised and reissued until 1962. Both the vocabulary included in the textbook and the sentences assigned for translation were based almost exclusively upon Caesar. "Terrified by the shouts, they betook themselves to the woods" (20, p. 37) and "Exhausted with wounds, they could not bear our charge" are fairly typical offerings (20, p. 47). Teachers familiar with the *Gallic Wars* will recognize the vocabulary and the sentence structure at once. More surprising, perhaps, is the degree to which even the *Fabulae Faciles* have been based upon Caesar. Yet John C. Kirtland's preface to the 1903 edition makes it clear that this work, too, was intended as preparation for reading the *Gallic Wars*.[5] Caesar was thus the one author who, because of his style, was deemed indispensable.

A similar impression may be gained from reading the preface to Charles E. Bennett's book on Latin prose composition, dating to 1912 and revised in 1919:

> Part I of the present work is based exclusively on Caesar. The illustrative examples are drawn directly from Caesar's own writings, either unchanged or with unessential alterations designed for practical use. The sentences of the Exercises bring into use only Caesar's vocabulary—chiefly the common words—and Caesar's constructions. (6, p. iii)

This work, like Ritchie's, continued to be reprinted until as recently as 1962 and is fairly similar to other Latin texts of the period. In all of these works, we see Latin being used as a vehicle for improving one's English vocabulary and style; and the model for improving that vocabulary and style was Caesar.

It is important, even today, that Latin teachers recognize this. For, once we understand that style more than any other factor caused Caesar to be included in the "standard Latin curriculum," the role and importance of the *Gallic Wars* becomes much clearer. The development of a disciplined and vigorous prose style, after all, is no less important today than it was when Ritchie's and Bennett's textbooks were written. Indeed, if, as has so often been heard, "students really are entering high school with far less background in 'traditional grammar' than they once had," then the importance of Caesar is even greater. For the *Gallic Wars* helps a class to understand that great complexities of grammar are not essential to a developed prose style. Even the simplest structures may be used to create prose that is elegant, crisp, and dynamic. In this way, the traditional approach to Caesar can illustrate for us how Caesar should be taught in classrooms today.

How to Use the *Gallic Wars* in the Classroom

The *Gallic Wars*, therefore, remains an appropriate vehicle for learning about expository prose. As the students read the text—paying attention to all the usual matters of vocabulary and grammar—they may be asked periodically to comment upon the style of a given passage. What do they observe about the length of the sentences or clauses? Is there an abundance of metaphors or other literary devices? Would they term Caesar's choice of words "practical" or does it seem to be more "poetic"? To further the students' understanding of these issues, the teacher may wish to assign a few English sentences that the students are to translate into "Caesarean Latin." At first, it is probably helpful to assign sentences that are only slight variants from the text of Caesar itself. For instance, in only the second chapter of the*Gallic Wars*, the students read the following statement about Orgetorix:

> *Id facilius eis persuasit, quod undique loci natura Helvetii continentur.*
> "He persuaded them of this more easily, because the Helvetians are hemmed in on all sides by the nature of the region." [1.2]

Once this passage has been studied, the teacher might assign a similar sentence such as "He persuaded them of this *quickly* because the *Sicilians* are hemmed in on all sides by *water*." (The italicized words are found in the glossaries of most textbooks.) Then, once the class has become comfortable with this relatively simple drill, the teacher may wish to select some more difficult examples from Ritchie's or Bennett's text (both still widely available in libraries) or to create new exercises. The class should be instructed that the goal of the assignment is not merely to translate the sentences into Latin, but also to imitate Caesar as closely as possible. What vocabulary might Caesar himself have chosen to express these thoughts? Which grammatical structures or idioms might he have used? How might several short sentences be joined together using subordinate clauses?

The objective in making this type of assignment is threefold. First, the mere process of translation will help the students to improve their mastery of Latin vocabulary and grammar; Latin will become for them an active skill, rather than the merely passive skill of reading. Second, the assignment will lead the students toward a greater appreciation of Caesar's unique vocabulary and style. Finally, the exercise will cause the students to reflect upon their own expository prose styles by forcing them to search for the simplest means of expression. As each of these assignments is completed, it is frequently useful to have the students write several of their sentences on a blackboard or overhead transparency. By comparing the work of other students with their own, the members of the class may discover alternative expressions for the same thought. They should be led to ask such questions as "What different means of conveying the same sentiment appear in these variant versions? What effect would be achieved by varying the order of the words? Can any of the sentences be simplified still further by eliminating unnecessary words or by choosing a less complicated vocabulary? Which sentences from the *Gallic Wars* itself seem most similar to the sentences found in the exercises?"

By completing projects of this kind, the class will develop a better understanding of the qualities to be found in the Caesarean style; they will form a clearer impression of the features they are trying to reproduce in their own sentences. To facilitate this process, the teacher might ask that the students list, from time to time, the most important qualities that they observe while reading Caesar's prose. What, the teacher might then continue, are the strengths of those qualities and what are their weaknesses? Where would this simple style of writing be most appropriate and where would it seem out of place? Are there authors who write in English with a style comparable to Caesar's? At the secondary level, it seems unlikely that the students will be able to name more than a very few English or American authors whose work seems stylistically comparable to Caesar. After posing this question, therefore, the teacher may wish to distribute selections from a novel or short story by Ernest Hemingway, an essay by E. B. White, the opening chapters of some modern detective fiction from the "hardboiled school," or the lead paragraphs of recent news stories. Since Hemingway is, without a doubt, the most important modern author of the "unadorned" style, the following lines from the end of *The Sun Also Rises* might be used to provide an interesting comparison to Caesar:

> Down-stairs we came out through the first-floor dining room to the street. A waiter went for a taxi. It was hot and bright. Up the street was a little square with trees and grass where there were taxis parked. A taxi came up the street, the waiter hanging out the side. I tipped him and told the driver where to drive, and got in beside Brett. The driver started up the street. I settled back. Brett moved close to me. We sat close against each other. (13, p. 247)

Or this passage, which opens the second chapter of *A Farewell to Arms:*

> The next year there were many victories. The mountain that was beyond the valley and the hillside where the chestnut forest grew was captured and there were victories beyond the plain on the plateau to the south and we crossed the river in August and lived in a house in Gorizia that had a fountain and many thick shady trees in a walled garden and a wistaria vine purple on the side of the house. Now the fighting was in the mountains and was not a mile away. The town was very nice. (12, p. 5)

After having been presented with passages such as these, the students might be divided into small groups to discuss them and to consider what, if anything, these passages have in common with Caesar's text. If the teacher wishes the students to compare the new material with a specific passage from Caesar, virtually any selection from the *Gallic Wars* will serve the purpose. But the teacher should recommend that the class review, in particular, the very opening of the *Gallic Wars*. This section will not only be quite fresh in the students' minds, but it also contains some of the clearest examples of the plain style likely to be found. Further samples of this style in Latin can be seen in the illustrative passage that appears in the *Auctor ad Herennium* 4.14.

As the teacher passes from group to group during this assignment, the students should be asked questions that direct their attention toward the most important features of each passage. Which elements, for instance, of Caesar's style produce an effect similar to Hemingway's short, almost abrupt, sentences? (This might be a good place to explain how

Latin often uses a clause where English would use a complete sentence.)
How would the students characterize Hemingway's choice of words? Are
there any parallels to this type of vocabulary in the text of Caesar? How
does Hemingway use "concrete" terms to create a vivid image in the mind
of the reader? How does Caesar achieve a similar effect? (If students have
difficulty answering the last question, invite them to read the *Gallic Wars*
7.77–78.)

At a later point in the semester, selected passages of Emerson,
Dickens, or Thomas Hardy might be presented in order to provide a
contrast to the plain and simple style of expository prose. The class should
be reminded that simple prose is not necessarily better than a more ornate
style; it is merely a type of writing that is more appropriate to certain types
of composition. The teacher might try composing an expository essay in
both the simple and ornate styles to illustrate this point. Afterwards, it
might be helpful for the teacher to assign the students essay topics for
compositions in which the English equivalent of the "Caesarean style" is
to be used. Suitable essay topics might include a description of a recent
sporting event, a retelling of a news story, summaries of ongoing political
debates, or a synopsis of a recent film. Once again, when this assignment is
complete, the students should examine selections from the essays that
have been written on the blackboard or on overhead transparencies. The
students themselves, by this time, should find it quite easy to discuss the
stylistic devices that they have used. During the course of this discussion,
they might be asked "What alternative phrasing can you suggest for this
idea? Are there words or phrases that can be omitted without significant
loss of meaning? Which sentences should be combined or, conversely, split
into smaller units? Are there expressions in the essays that have equivalents in Caesarean Latin?"

It is frequently useful to end this exercise by showing the class how
not to imitate the style of the *Gallic Wars*. For instance, Russell Baker's
"Caesar's Puerile Wars" is a humorous essay in which the young Julius
Caesar is imagined to be faced with that inevitable composition topic:
"How I Spent My Summer Vacation." Master "Caesar" then proceeds to
demonstrate all the least attractive features of his later writing style and, in
so doing, Baker manages to capture the flavor of the "all too literal"
student translation:

> These things thus being so which also, from the nones to the ides, the
> impediments having been abandoned, Caesar constituted on the rostrum to

exhort his comrades to joy. "No more lessons, no more parchment scrolls, no more teacher's dirty looks," Caesar hortated. (5, p. 27)

Though it can serve primarily as light relief at the end of this assignment, Baker's essay also makes an important point about the Caesarean style. To illustrate this point, the students might be asked, for example, "Which features of Baker's intentionally awkward phrasing are designed to imitate the style of the *Gallic Wars?* How do these features illustrate the differences between Caesarean Latin and current taste in expository prose style? What are the more acceptable English equivalents to Caesar's frequent use of participles and the ablative absolute?" A discussion of such issues as these will encourage students not only to see the importance of a smooth and flowing style, but also to avoid translating each word of Latin into its strict English equivalent.

Additional Roles for Caesar in the Curriculum

In this way, we have seen that Caesar's place in the "standard Latin curriculum" resulted at least as much from his style as from his content. But, in any age, it proves impossible to read an author solely as a stylistic model. Sooner or later attention must be given to what an author is saying as well as how he has chosen to say it. In the British public schools of the late nineteenth and early twentieth centuries, the task of "interpreting Caesar" was readily accomplished; the parallel courses of the British and Roman empires made comparisons between the two all but inescapable. Caesar and Cicero could thus be read as the two voices of "Empire"—as textbooks in military and political duty, respectively—and their narratives could be treated as object lessons for a later colonial power.

Even in our own country, the works of Caesar were, until fairly recently, treated merely as sourcebooks in strategy and as collections of lessons in personal courage. For instance, Ullman and Henry's Intermediate Latin texts, widely used throughout the 1960s, summarized the importance of Caesar and of the *Gallic Wars* in these words:

Caesar...was one of the military geniuses of history, ranking with Alexander, Hannibal, Scipio, and Napoleon. He was a very great statesman. His military successes and his political activities profoundly affected the future of the world....In 1939 the United States Army returned to a system of drill movements very much like that of the Roman army. The advantages are simplicity and maneuverability. (25, pp. 184–85)

The implication, of course, is that Caesar's influence still may be felt in the military sphere. The importance of Caesar is reduced to that of a military "genius" and the *Gallic Wars* may be read as providing examples of his strategy. Hines and Welch, another popular text of the same period, makes a similar point and then goes further:

> It is not merely a history of warfare that Caesar has given us. He has written stirring tales of personal heroism, of characters noble or base, and of peoples, of places, of customs strange and unique. It is an account of the early inhabitants of Western Europe and is one of the earliest sources of information regarding that part of the world. (14, p. 190)

The treatment of the *Gallic Wars* in most American schools, therefore, became something of a travelogue compounded with an apologue: Marco Polo meets John Bunyan. Perhaps for this reason, texts of this period almost always contained two particular incidents from the *Gallic Wars*, no matter how much other text they may have omitted: the description of the culture found among the Gauls and the Germans [6.11–27: the travelogue] and the competition between the centurions Pullo and Vorenus for greater glory [5.44: the apologue].

The textbooks that contain these passages, and the traditional interpretations of them, are still being used in many American classrooms. To some extent, therefore, the cause of much of the current opposition to Caesar is not a function of the text; it is a function of the textbook. It is the approach to Caesar that many teachers find objectionable.

New Approaches to Teaching the *Gallic Wars*

The solution to this problem, of course, is not to abandon Caesar himself but to develop a new approach to the *Gallic Wars*. This approach should be one that fulfills the teacher's own educational objectives and achieves the goals of the current curriculum. Since these goals and objectives will vary from teacher to teacher—and even from class to class for the same teacher—it is not possible to outline one approach to Caesar that will suit every purpose. But it may be useful to examine a few of the most common approaches that can be taken toward Caesar in order to provide the teacher with additional ideas. The first of these methods is merely a variant of that already found in most existing textbooks; the others will require substantially more innovation and preparation on the part of the teacher. Moreover, it should be noted that the list that follows is in no way intended to be comprehensive or to imply that the various approaches are mutually exclusive. Our primary goal, rather, should be to survey the sorts of things that might be done in an Intermediate Latin course in order to provide the unit on Caesar with a unifying theme.

The Biographical Approach

The first way of approaching the *Gallic Wars*, therefore, is to see it as providing insight into one of the pivotal figures of world history. Whether we regard Caesar as a military genius or as a political tyrant, after all, "Few men in the history of the world have had more to do with the making of modern civilization than Julius Caesar" (Hines and Welch, 14, p. 186). For this reason, the teacher may focus the material of the Intermediate Latin course upon the figure of Caesar himself. What, in other words, made this particular Roman statesman and general so important? And what can we learn from a study of his life and times?

Any attempt to answer this question, of course, cannot limit itself to the bare, factual matter of what Caesar did; it should also touch upon the issue of why certain individuals exert extraordinary influence. This is the approach that used to be known as the "Great Man" school of history. Is there any effect, the students should be asked, that individuals can have upon world events? Or was Caesar's eminence merely an accident of the time? Did his influence arise out of the power of his personality or were larger social forces at work?

In addressing these issues, students should be encouraged to look beyond the *Gallic Wars* for sources of material. They should be asked to compare the image of Caesar that emerges from his own writings with that found in Cicero's letters, Suetonius's or Plutarch's *Life of Caesar*, Appian's history of the Civil Wars, Shakespeare's *Julius Caesar*, and Shaw's *Caesar and Cleopatra*. One convenient source for all of these materials, as well as a useful list of discussion and paper topics and additional bibliography, was published by G. B. Harrison (11) in 1960; this volume is still available in many libraries. A briefer—and, unfortunately, more "dated"—exposure to several of these sources may be found in the 1964 CBS/BFA film entitled *Four Views of Caesar* (10).

Students who have read or watched these other accounts of Caesar's life develop both a greater appreciation for the literary qualities of the

Gallic Wars and a more complete view of Caesar as a historical figure. With certain classes, the teacher may wish to compare the character of Caesar to other "great figures" from the past, including Alexander the Great (whom Plutarch paired, after all, with Caesar in the *Parallel Lives*), Pericles, Cleopatra, Hannibal, and Napoleon. These figures, too, tend to be treated by a number of authors in novels, stories, plays, films, and essays. It is thus possible, for instance, to arrange a discussion of the different historical interpretations of Cleopatra in light of the different interpretations of Caesar. This type of assignment will lead the class to consider the historical and personal forces that surrounded each of these characters individually. Furthermore, they will see how an author must select from among these historical and personal forces when presenting a coherent literary profile.

The Historical Approach

Another way of reading the *Gallic Wars* would be to treat it as a primary source for information about what is, beyond any doubt, the most dramatic era in Roman history: the period of the Roman revolution. No one would expect, of course, a student in a high school Latin class to have read Ronald Syme's monumental work on this period; but some of the issues raised by Syme may be broached through a study of Caesar himself. The teacher of the course will need to provide the students with many of the facts surrounding the Roman revolution. This might be done by ending certain class periods—perhaps those in which grammar is reviewed during the first quarter of the year—with "minilectures" about the social impact of the Second Punic War, the reforms of the Gracchi, the Land Commission, Marius and Sulla, and the origins of First Triumvirate. Many Intermediate Latin textbooks contain short readings, either in Latin or English, on these very topics.

After this historical outline has been presented, the students might be asked such questions as "Which social factors seem to have made Rome ripe for change in this period? What demands were made by the social reformers and how were these demands received by others in Rome? Why did certain of the Romans believe that the senatorial system had become too inefficient to govern an expanding empire?" The teacher may also wish to draw historical parallels between the social conditions that led to revolution in Rome and those that led to similar struggles in America, France, and Russia.

Furthermore, the events that occurred during the Roman revolution may be brought to life for students by exposing them to some of the historical novels that focus on Caesar's life. Most libraries either have or can readily obtain copies of such novels as Paul L. Anderson's *Pugnax the Gladiator* (1), *A Slave of Catiline* (2), *Swords in the North* (3), and *With the Eagles* (4); Mary Machado's *In Caesar's Shadow* (18);[6] Rex Warner's *The Young Caesar* (27) and *Imperial Caesar* (26); Thornton Wilder's *The Ides of March* (28); and John Williams's *Augustus* (29). These novels present much of the same information students would find in a standard historical summary. But they present the information in a way that will bring the characters of the period to life for students and will increase their appreciation for the political issues behind the *Gallic Wars*. By using this approach, therefore, teachers will discover that they have numerous opportunities for discussing the *Gallic Wars* as a work of literature. Distinguishing, for example, between Caesar's literary objectives and those of the historical novelist would help, in the end, to bring both into a clearer focus.

The Ethnographic Approach

A third way of studying the *Gallic Wars* is to examine the text as a source of sociological and cultural material. This is a particularly fruitful approach since, in the course of describing various campaigns, Caesar will frequently discuss the customs of the peoples involved; he also provides insight into the daily life of the Romans themselves. Each student in the class, therefore, might be assigned some aspect of cultural ethnography— for example, the description of a people's religious beliefs, political system, class structure, military technique, marriage rites, or folklore— and then be expected to provide periodic reports on this topic throughout the semester.

Some of these topics—the report on marriage rites, for instance—are small enough that it might be possible for the same student to conduct research into both the Gallic customs and their Roman equivalents. Other topics are so broad that students should be encouraged to "specialize" in one of these two cultures. In either case, however, by hearing reports on the differences between Gallic and Roman tradition, the students will come to recognize the unique features of each. The students should also be encouraged to consider such issues as how these differences in culture and tradition may have developed; whether certain customs and habits are manifestly "superior" to others or whether different cultures simply suit the divergent needs of different peoples; what attitudes the Romans and the Gauls took toward the different social customs of the other. (As a means of incorporating both the "Biographical" and the "Ethnographic" approaches into the same course, the teacher may wish to consider how Caesar interpreted cultural differences among peoples in comparison to how other ancient figures—for instance, a general like Alexander the Great or a historian like Herodotus—explained and regarded such differences.)

Students should be asked to research these reports, not only in a primary source such as the *Gallic Wars*, but also in such works as Anne Ross's *Everyday Life of the Pagan Celts* (23), Jérôme Carcopino's *Daily Life in Ancient Rome* (8), and F. R. Cowell's *Life in Ancient Rome* (9). If the students live in a community where a major museum is located, it may be possible for them to take a field trip in order to examine some of the artifacts left behind by these and other early cultures. Where such facilities are not available, the teacher may wish to "illustrate" the students' reports by means of slides, circulating texts, or museum replicas. Whichever of these methods the teacher may use, however, the students will be better able to visualize the events they encounter in Caesar and to see his text as dealing with the struggles and aspirations of "real people."

Conclusion

There are, of course, many other approaches the teacher may take. (See, for instance, Mench, 19.) Caesar may be studied as a propagandist, a military theorist, a political reformer, a tyrant, or a heroic failure. He may also, as we saw earlier, be read for the insight he provides into the causes of war. But, whichever of these approaches the teacher may adopt, it should always be combined, at least to some extent, with the traditional use of Caesar as a stylistic model. By combining two approaches in this way, the teacher will introduce the students both to the expository style of one of Rome's greatest authors and to a few simple techniques of literary interpretation. The first approach will help the students to improve their understanding of Latin (and English) grammar, vocabulary, and style; the second approach will explore how these same linguistic elements may be used to achieve a particular literary end.

Students who begin such a course by seeing Latin merely as a linguistic "puzzle" to be solved will end the year with a greater understanding, not only of the *Gallic Wars*, but of literature as a whole. The results of this technique will be improvement in the student's own expository style and in his or her ability to appreciate the written works of major authors. And now, *alea iacta est.*

Notes

1. For a more complete discussion of "Atticism" and "Neo-Atticism," see Kennedy (16, pp. 330–36, and 17, pp. 241–46).
2. These phrases are taken from Harry Caplan's translation of the famous definition of the "plain style" [adtenuata figura] in the *Auctor ad Herennium* (7, pp. 253 and 261). The original Latin text reads *"Adtenuata est quae demissa est usque ad usitatissimam puri consuetudinem sermonis"* [4.11] and *"id quod ad infimum et cotidianum sermonem demissum est"* [4.14].
3. A number of Ritchie's stories still appear in current texts. For example, Ritchie's famous account of the labors of Hercules and his version of the legend of the Argonauts are used as introductory units in Jenney (15).
4. Indeed, Ritchie's original title for his composition text indicates even more clearly the focus of the work: **Imitative Exercises in Easy Latin Prose** [emphasis added].
5. For instance, references to "the Latinity of Caesar," "the large use of Caesarian words and phrases," and "the study of Nepos or Caesar" appear throughout Kirtland's preface.
6. These first five novels have recently been reissued and are available through the Teaching Materials and Resource Center of the American Classical League (Miami University, Oxford, Ohio 45056).

References

1. Anderson, Paul L. *Pugnax the Gladiator.* New York: Biblo and Tannen, 1959.
2. _____. *A Slave of Catiline.* New York: Biblo and Tannen, 1971.
3. _____. *Swords in the North.* New York: Biblo and Tannen, 1968.
4. _____. *With the Eagles.* New York: Biblo and Tannen, 1972.
5. Baker, Russell. "Caesar's Puerile Wars," pp. 27–29 in *So This Is Depravity.* New York: Washington Square Press, 1981.
6. Bennett, Charles E. *A New Latin Composition.* Rev. ed. New York: Allyn and Bacon, 1919.
7. Caplan, Harry, ed. and trans. *[Cicero] Ad C. Herennium.* Cambridge, MA: Harvard University Press, 1977.
8. Carcopino, Jérôme. *Daily Life in Ancient Rome.* New Haven, CT: Yale University Press, 1940.
9. Cowell, F. R. *Life in Ancient Rome.* New York: Perigee, 1961.
10. *Four Views of Caesar.* New York: CBS/BFA Films, 1964. [22 minutes, black and white]
11. Harrison, G. B. *Julius Caesar in Shakespeare, Shaw and the Ancients.* New York: Harcourt, Brace and World, 1960.
12. Hemingway, Ernest. *A Farewell to Arms.* New York: Scribner's, 1929.
13. _____. *The Sun Also Rises.* New York: Scribner's, 1926.
14. Hines, Therese, and Edward J. Welch. *Our Latin Heritage.* Book II. New York: Harcourt, Brace and World, 1966.
15. Jenney, Charles. *Jenney's Second Year Latin.* Revised by R. V. Scudder, E. C. Baade, and D. C. Coffin. New York: Allyn and Bacon, 1984.
16. Kennedy, George. *The Art of Persuasion in Greece.* Princeton, NJ: Princeton University Press, 1963.
17. _____. *The Art of Rhetoric in the Roman World.* Princeton, NJ: Princeton University Press, 1972.
18. Machado, Mary. *In Caesar's Shadow.* Elizabeth, NJ: American Press, 1975.
19. Mench, Fred. *Caesar in the Curriculum—Some New Approaches.* Miami, OH: American Classical League, 1985.

20. Ritchie, Francis. *Exercises in Latin Prose Composition*. Revised by J. W. Bartram. New York: David McKay, 1938.
21. _____. *Ritchie's Fabulae Faciles: A First Latin Reader*. Edited and adapted by John Copeland Kirtland. New York: Longman, 1903.
22. Rose, H. J. *A Handbook of Latin Literature*. New York: Dutton, 1960.
23. Ross, Anne. *Everyday Life of the Pagan Celts*. London: Carousel, 1972.
24. Scottish Classics Group. *Ecce Romani*. American Edition. New York: Longman, 1984.
25. Ullman, B. L., and Norman E. Henry. *Latin for Americans*. Second Book. New York: Macmillan, 1959.
26. Warner, Rex. *Imperial Caesar*. New York: Little, Brown, 1960.
27. _____. *The Young Caesar*. New York: Little, Brown, 1958.
28. Wilder, Thornton. *The Ides of March*. New York: Harper, 1948.
29. Williams, John. *Augustus*. New York: Viking, 1972.

10
Cracking the Code: Helping Students with Specific Learning Disabilities

Bettye J. Myer
Miami University, Oxford, Ohio
Leonore Ganschow
Miami University, Oxford, Ohio
Richard Sparks
College of Mount Saint Joseph on the Ohio, Cincinnati, Ohio
Sylvia Kenneweg
Hathaway Brown School, Shaker Heights, Ohio

How can we help them learn? This is an important question when considering curriculum for any student, but it is especially compelling when approaching the teaching-learning situation for students with learning difficulties. Increasingly, student populations in second language classrooms represent a diverse range of aptitude and ability for language learning. The state of North Carolina is the first in the nation to require that K–5 second language study be provided for every child in the state, beginning in 1993, according to Senate Bill 1 of North Carolina's Appropriations Act (Toussaint, 20). As units of government such as North Carolina and New York City mandate second language study for all students at selected levels, and as a growing population of students identified as having specific learning disabilities (SLD) opt for a college-bound course of study, responsive language teachers at all levels will seek answers to methodological questions about how best to instruct their students. Are there methodologies that are helpful to students who experience learning difficulties in certain teaching-learning situations?

BUSINESS REPLY MAIL

FIRST CLASS   PERMIT NO. 14407   CHICAGO, IL

POSTAGE WILL BE PAID BY ADDRESSEE

National Textbook Company
a division of *NTC Publishing Group*

4255 West Touhy Avenue

Lincolnwood, Illinois 60646-1975

The ACTFL Free Examination Plan

Each year the American Council on the Teaching of Foreign Languages and National Textbook Company publish the definitive work on the key issue affecting the foreign language teaching profession. This year's publication is basic reading for everyone involved in foreign language education.

YES, I want to receive the annual ACTFL publication. I understand that once each year (November) I will receive the new annual publication with invoice. I will have 30 days to examine the book and decide whether to keep it or return it. I may remove my name from the Free Examination Plan at any time upon request without charge or penalty.

Modern
Technology in
Foreign
Language
Education:
Applications
and Projects

Wm. Flint Smith
Editor

The ACTFL Foreign Language Education Series

Published by National Textbook Company
in cooperation with the American Council on the Teaching of Foreign Languages

The Plan enables you to receive the annual publication on a priority basis each year and enjoy these benefits:

✓ **Free examination of the new book the moment it comes off the press**

✓ **Special Free Examination Plan price** (Save 20% on each new book)

✓ **Full return privilege for 30 days**

✓ **The right to drop the Plan at any time at your request**

The ACTFL Free Examination Plan is your assurance that your professional bookshelf never goes out of date. Sign up today!

Name_____

School Name and Address_____
(if applicable)

Shipping Address_____

City_____ State_____ Zip_____

Billing Address (if different)_____

City_____ State_____ Zip_____

Authorized Signature_____

Salesperson's Signature_____

Purchase Order No. (if needed)_____

Date_____

Telephone (___)_____

Each year ship me _____ copies of the annual ACTFL publication in paperback.

BR2294

Any attempt to respond risks oversimplifying a very complex issue. Yet there do seem to be approaches to second language learning that benefit students with language difficulties. The success of immersion school settings for children with learning disabilities in Canada has been discussed by Cummins (4). A few secondary schools are addressing the issue through classes designed for students who have been identified as being at risk for second language learning in regular classes. Two Ohio schools have initiated such programs. Kenneweg of Hathaway Brown School in Shaker Heights, Ohio, has modified the Orton-Gillingham approach to teaching reading and spelling in English for her Spanish O-G classes with success for the past nine years. At Worthington High School in Worthington, Ohio, two Spanish courses (Level 1 and Level 2) are being offered during the 1988–89 school year for students who are at risk for language learning (5). In both instances, teachers have devised multi-sensory approaches to teaching these classes, emphasizing the integration of listening, speaking, reading, writing, and visual support of a pictorial and verbal nature.

At the university level, support for students with learning difficulties who are studying a second language is offered most frequently through a tutoring system. (In a few instances, individualized pacing and special courses are provided.) Questionnaire results from 105 institutions of higher education indicated that 74 percent provide tutoring that is either partially or totally funded by the institution (Ganschow, Myer, and Roeger, 6). At the postsecondary level it is perhaps through a tutoring system or in an individualized setting that students with learning disabilities will best make progress toward cracking the language code.

For most teachers, a full-class approach is the only viable option for addressing the needs of the diverse abilities that are represented in our classrooms. Instruction that places a heavy emphasis on oral communication may pose serious problems for the students who have language-learning difficulties. The present authors would like to focus attention on a remedial approach that has traditionally been used in a one-to-one setting for instructing students who have serious phonological problems in English-language learning. Because of having a phonological deficit, some students may find that the written code or the spoken language may remain a secret code in a typical full-class setting.

The purpose of this article is threefold: (1) to provide a brief introduction to the nature of a phonological disability that is characteristic of a select group—students with specific learning disabilities (SLD); (2) to describe the Orton-Gillingham (O-G) remedial approach to teaching the sound system of the English language and its relationship to written English; and, (3) to demonstrate how this approach might be applied to the teaching of a second language in remedial tutorial settings.

Phonological Disabilities

Evidence supporting the existence of phonological disabilities comes primarily from research on the identification of patterns or "subtypes" within the SLD population. SLD students have been found to differ significantly from one another in the patterns of learning difficulties that they represent (Boder, 2; Lyon, 14; Mattis, French, and Rapin, 15; McKinney, 16; Rourke, 17). There is consensus among educators today that students with specific learning disabilities are a heterogeneous and complex group (Lovett, 13; McKinney, 16). Within the literature of subtypes of learning disabilities is a *pattern* of language/reading disorders commonly called a phonological disability.

Phonology is the science of speech sounds, i.e., abstract signal elements that are presented by the sounds of speech. Phonics is a method of reading instruction designed to help the child see that words have an internal phonological structure (Liberman, 11). Liberman explains phonology in the following example:

> [T]hough the word "bag" has three phonological units, and correspondingly, three letters in print, it has only one pulse of sound: the three elements of the underlying phonological structure—the three phonemes—have been thoroughly overlapped and merged into that one sound—"bag" (p. 2).

Students with Phonological Disabilities

Students with phonological disabilities are unable to make the linkage between the word they hear (i.e., bag) and the phonological units within the word (b-a-g). In other words, they can't break down words into sounds. Many also have difficulty putting individual sounds together (b-r-a-g = brag), some cannot break down words into syllables (el-e-phant). Most have problems when asked to sequence the sounds of a word in order. For example, b-a-r-t for b-r-a-t suggests confusion about the sequence of sounds. Additional characteristics of students with phono-logical disabilities may be found in Figure 1. All of these phonological problems indicate a lack of metalinguistic awareness, which is essential to the acquisition of alphabetic literacy (Liberman, 11, p. 3). Metalinguistic awareness refers to the conscious attention to language elements, or the ability to manipulate language as an object (Bialystok and Ryan, 1). Students who lack phonological awareness are unable to recognize the relationships between the sound components of the language. Metalin-guistic deficiencies in phonological understanding are said to occur in people of all ages and cultural backgrounds (Liberman, 11).

Figure 1

Characteristics of Students with Phonological Processing Deficits*

- Difficulty with oral expression
- Difficulty with listening comprehension
- Early history of articulation difficulties and/or delayed language
- Difficulty putting sounds together to form words when reading
- Difficulty in sound–symbol correspondence (i.e., relating phonemes and graphemes)
- Poor awareness of phonological and syllabic structure of spoken language
- Inability to segment spoken words into phonemes and syllables
- Inefficient word decoding
- Poor spelling
- Overreliance on visual memory for word recognition
- Poor reading comprehension due to inability to "crack the code"
- No impairment in visual processing ability
- Short-term memory deficits for material that can be coded verbally but long-term memory organization apparently intact
- Intact ability to use context for word recognition

*A student may not necessarily exhibit all these characteristics.

One remedial strategy for teaching beginning reading, writing, and spelling to students with severe phonological processing deficits is to provide direct and explicit teaching of the sound system of spoken language and its relationship to written language. Numerous remedial education programs have been developed to assist teachers in helping SLD students "crack the written language code." Among others, these include Orton-Gillingham (Gillingham and Stillman, 7; Orton, 18), Alpha-betic Phonics (Cox, 3), Auditory Discrimination in Depth (Lindamood and Lindamood, 12), Project Read (Green and Enfield, 8; 9), Recipe for

Reading (Traub and Bloom, 21), and the Slingerland program (Slingerland, 19).

The Orton-Gillingham (O-G) method adheres to a direct and explicit teaching of phonics in a highly structured, step-by-step procedure. A small amount of material is presented at one time; mastery through multisensory practice, presentation, and review are critical to the success of the method. Student progress is carefully monitored at every step.

The multisensory approach distinguishes this method from many methods of language instruction. Initially, letters that represent the single sounds (phonograms) of familiar speech are presented to students. Then the single sounds are immediately synthesized into meaningful words. By introducing the phonograms through a multisensory means of input, i.e., hearing (auditory); seeing (visual); and feeling through articulation, touch, and arm movement (tactile-kinesthetic), students are provided the advantage of input through several senses. In this way, a weakness in any one learning pathway may be less a hindrance because it is not the only means for gaining information. Careful pacing, structured procedures, and a sequential presentation that combines reading, spelling, and writing help students to succeed.

The Orton-Gillingham (O-G) Method

Each new letter or letter combination, and its sound, is taught by the following process:

1. Show a card to students with the phonogram, along with a picture whose initial sound begins with this phonogram. The picture helps them to associate the phonogram with a concrete object. It should be left within visual range of the students.
2. Give the sound of the phonogram to the students.
3. Have the students repeat the phonogram clearly.
4. Write the phonogram on paper, a blackboard, or an erasable surface (magic slate).
5. Have the students say the sound aloud as they simultaneously trace the letter(s). Do this three times.
6. Have the students copy the letter(s) as they simultaneously say the sound. Do this three times. Discuss mouth or tongue positions, involvement of vocal cords, or any other useful kinesthetic clue.

7. Reinforce the use of the visual (referred to in the O-G literature as a "catch word") to assist in retrieving the sound. Discuss the position of the phonogram in the word if applicable, e.g., "ey" has an ending position.

8. Give the students a list of words to read composed of this phonogram and other phonograms that they have learned. (Do not give words with phonograms that the students have not learned.) Vowels may be written in red so that they are emphasized.

9. Dictate a list of spelling words to be written. All of the words should contain only this phonogram and other phonograms that they have learned.

10. Dictate sentences for the students to write with words containing the new phonogram and previously learned phonograms. Non-phonetic sight words that have been learned by the student may be included (e.g., *the, of, was*).

11. Present the card with the new phonogram for review and ask the students to give the sound and "catch word."

12. Add the new phonogram card to a deck of phonograms previously learned by the students. The students should practice this deck of phonograms daily. The teacher presents the phonograms and the students respond by giving the sound. Then the teacher gives the sound and the students respond be repeating the sound as they write the letter(s).

Example in French

1. Show a card to the students with the phonogram and a picture whose initial sound begins with this phonogram. Leave it within the visual range of the students.
   CHAT (picture of cat)

2. Give the sound of the phonogram to the students. [ʃ]

3. Have the students repeat the phonogram clearly. [ʃ]

4. Write the phonogram on paper, blackboard, etc. [CH]

5. The students say the sound aloud as they trace the letters three times.
   [ʃ] + trace letters over card (three times)

6. The students copy the letters as they say the sound. Do this three times. Discuss tongue vibration, no involvement of vocal cords.
   [ʃ] + write the letters (three times)

7. Reinforce the use of the visual ("catch word") with the students to assist in retrieving the sound. The teacher could use an illustration of a cat dancing.
   CHAT CHAT CHAT (dance rhythm imitating the CHA-CHA)
8. The students read a list of words that have this phonogram in combination with other phonograms that have been learned. (Do not give words with phonograms that the students have not learned.) Vowels are written in red.
   Printed word CHAT + illustration of a cat
   Printed word CHOU + illustration of a cream puff or cabbage
   Printed word CHIEN + illustration of a dog
   Printed word CHAISE + illustration of a chair
   Printed word CHAINE + illustration of a chain
   Printed word CHANT + illustration of rooster singing
9. Dictate the six words from the list for the students to spell on paper:
   CHAT
   CHOU
   CHIEN
   CHAISE
   CHAINE
   CHANT
10. Dictate sentences to the students with words containing the new phonogram and previously learned phonograms.
    LE CHOU EST BON.
    LE CHIEN EST BEAU.
    LE CHAT EST BON.
11. Present the card with the new phonogram for review and ask the students to give the sound and "catch word."
12. Add the new phonogram card to a deck of phonograms previously learned by the students. The students should practice this deck of phonograms daily. The teacher presents each phonogram and the students respond by giving the sound. Then the teacher gives the sound and the students respond by repeating the sound as they write the letter(s).

The above descriptions of teaching phonograms represent a highly structured approach that links sound and written representations. By following this approach, it is hypothesized that mastery of individual sounds and their written forms can be attained by most students.

Conclusion

Students with phonological deficits will meet roadblocks to successful foreign language learning. A first obstacle: Foreign language teachers have not been trained either to identify or to work with students with specific learning disabilities. Second, foreign language teachers do not have the time to provide the extensive remedial, individualized instruction that is required for SLD students to "crack the code." Third, there are no basic foreign language materials comparable to the remedial educational programs designed for at-risk native language learners. At the present time, there is no research evidence to suggest that remedial instruction on "cracking the code" of a foreign language will help students with phonological deficits learn the language.

Can an O-G approach be adapted to learning a foreign language? Though this approach has not been commonly used in foreign language classrooms, it has been tried and found to be successful for several years in the classes of one of the present authors, Kenneweg. In a recent article on the O-G approach (Kenneweg, 10), she describes how she has incorporated O-G methods in full-class instruction. The techniques include multisensory input, the careful sequencing of materials, controlled pacing of presentations, oral practice and board drills, flash cards and filmstrips, and the integration of reading, spelling, and writing.

The O-G method is an approach to teaching the decoding and encoding of written language. Perhaps for a select group of foreign language learners—SLD students with phonological disabilities— teachers should consider supplementing or replacing traditional approaches to second language learning. Learning to read and write in the second language prior to oral communication may be a more effective way to "crack the code" for some students.

References

1. Bialystok, Ellen, and Ellen Bouchard Ryan. "A Metacognitive Framework for the Development of First and Second Language Skills," pp. 207–51 in D. L. Forrest-Pressley, G. E. MacKinnon, and T. G. Waller, eds., *Metacognition, Cognition, and Human Performance.* Volume 1. New York: Academic Press, 1985.
2. Boder, Eleanor. "Developmental Dyslexia: A Diagnostic Approach Based on Three Typical Reading-Spelling Patterns." *Developmental Medicine and Child Neurology* 15 (1973):663–87.

3. Cox, A. R. "Alphabetic Phonics: An Organization and Expansion of Orton-Gillingham." *Annals of Dyslexia* 35 (1985):187–98.
4. Cummins, Jim. *Bilingualism and Special Education: Issues in Assessment and Pedagogy.* Clevedon, England: Multilingual Matters, 1984.
5. Davis, Jo Dee. Personal communication, 1988.
6. Ganschow, Leonore, Bettye Myer, and Kathy Roeger. "Foreign Language Policies and Procedures for Students with Specific Learning Disabilities." [Paper submitted for publication, 1988.]
7. Gillingham, Anna, and Bessie Stillman. *Remedial Training for Children with Specific Disability in Reading, Spelling, and Penmanship.* Cambridge, MA: Educators Publishing Service, 1968.
8. Greene, Victoria, and Mary Lee Enfield. *Project Read Reading Guide: Phase I.* Bloomington, MN: Bloomington Public Schools, 1985.
9. _____. *Project Read Reading Guide: Phase II.* Bloomington, MN: Bloomington Public Schools, 1985.
10. Kenneweg, Sylvia. "Meeting Special Learning Needs in the Spanish Curriculum of a College Preparatory School," pp. 16–18 in Barbara Snyder, ed., *Get Ready, Get Set, Go! Action in the Foreign Language Classroom.* The Ohio Foreign Language Association Journal, 1988.
11. Liberman, Isabelle Y. "Language and Literacy: The Obligation of the Schools of Education," in *Intimacy with Language: A Forgotten Basic in Teacher Education.* Proceedings of the Orton Dyslexia Society Symposium. Baltimore: The Orton Dyslexia Society, 1987.
12. Lindamood, C. H., and P. C. Lindamood. *The A.D.D. Program: Auditory Discrimination in Depth.* Books 1 and 2. Hingham, MA: Teaching Resources, 1975.
13. Lovett, Maureen W. "The Search for Subtypes of Specific Reading Disability: Reflections from a Cognitive Perspective." *Annals of Dyslexia* 34 (1984):155–78.
14. Lyon, G. Reid. "Identification and Remediation of Learning Disability Subtypes: Preliminary Findings." *Learning Disabilities Focus* 1, 1 (1985):11–35.
15. Mattis, S., J. H. French, and I. Rapin. "Dyslexia in Children and Young Adults: Three Independent Neuropsychological Syndromes." *Developmental Medicine and Child Neurology* 17 (1975):150–63.
16. McKinney, James D. "The Search for Subtypes of Specific Learning Disability." *Journal of Learning Disabilities* 17, 1 (1984):43–50.
17. Rourke, Byron P., ed., *Neuropsychology of Learning Disabilities: Essentials of Subtype Analysis.* New York: Guilford, 1985.
18. Orton, J. A. "The Orton-Gillingham Approach," pp. 119–46 in J. Money, ed., *The Disabled Reader.* Baltimore: Johns Hopkins University Press, 1966.
19. Slingerland, B. H. *A Multisensory Approach to Language Arts for Specific Language Disability in Children: A Guide for Primary Teachers.* Cambridge, MA: Educators Publishing Service, 1971.
20. Toussaint, L. Gerard. Personal communication, 1988.
21. Traub, N., and F. Bloom. *Recipe for Reading.* Cambridge, MA: Educators Publishing Service, 1975.

11
Implementation of "Learning Cycles" in a Civilization Course: A Methodological Approach

Nicole Fouletier-Smith
University of Nebraska –Lincoln

Since the early 1980s language teaching in the United States has been reevaluated in the light of the proficiency concept. Levels of proficiency in speaking a language have been established, based on specific criteria (ETS, 7). Work has started as well on defining levels of cultural proficiency, or cultural competency as it is also called (ACTFL, 1).

Several ways to measure cultural competency have been suggested (e.g., Allen, 2) and contested (e.g., Knox, 12) but the question of how to impart cultural competence to learners continues to be an important topic: for some educators, contrastive analysis (e.g., Brière, 3) is the key, for others an anthropological perspective (e.g., Debyser, 5) ought to be adopted, and still others indicate that if history and art history have lost their supremacy in the culture class, they should not be completely sacrificed (Carr, 4). What follows is an alternative model for the teaching of civilization based on a tool used with good success at the University of Nebraska–Lincoln in teaching history, anthropology, English, and physics: the concept of the "learning cycle."

The Learning Cycle: A Classroom Instruction Strategy

The term "learning cycle" was first used by physicist R. Karplus (10). Based upon the work of Piaget, the learning cycle is described by Karplus as a classroom instruction strategy with the goal of promoting active learning by the students. This interpretation of Piaget's theory of human intellectual development (Inhelder and Piaget, 9) focuses on the last two stages of logical operations, concrete and formal thought, which are particularly relevant to college-age students. Karplus reminds us that "Piaget has ascribed the process whereby individuals advance from one stage to the next to four contributing factors: maturation, experience with the physical environment, social transmission and 'equilibration.' This last item designates an internal mental process in which new experiences are combined with prior expectations and generate new logical operations" (11, p. 170). Karplus notes that he substitutes the term "self-regulation" for "equilibration" because it has fewer science connotations and emphasizes the active role played by individuals. His learning cycle, therefore, consists of "three instructional phases that combine experience with social transmissions and encourages self-regulation" (11, p. 173).

The discovery of Karplus's work and its subsequent applications by a professor of French civilization was facilitated by an intermediary, Robert Fuller, physics professor at the University of Nebraska–Lincoln. Fuller was a leading participant in an interdisciplinary group of University of Nebraska–Lincoln professors who, in the early 70s, became interested in the works of Piaget and also in the newly published scheme of Perry (14). In 1975, a project took shape and an Exxon Foundation grant funded the program ADAPT (Accents on Developing Abstract Processes of Thought). This Piagetian-based multidisciplinary freshman program has become a model for similar programs across the country and Fuller is today recognized as one of the outstanding educators in America.

The ADAPT Program

Because the ADAPT program is interdisciplinary, the Karplus model of learning cycles was slightly modified (Fuller, 8) by the ADAPT faculty to fit disciplines other than physics (for example, English, history, anthropology). Like the Karplus model, the ADAPT learning cycle distinguishes three phases in learning, which follow each other chronologically. They are described briefly below, the Karplus term being given in parentheses.

Exploration (Karplus: Exploration)   This is a very open-ended student activity. With or without the instructor's broad questioning, but prompted by his/her suggestions and encouragements, students recall and share past concrete experiences on a given topic.

Invention (Karplus: Concept Introduction)   During this phase, the concrete experiences related during the exploration are analyzed as the basis for classification, possible generalization, and hypothesizing.

Application (Karplus: Concept Application)   At this final stage, students are encouraged to verify ventured hypotheses and thus broaden their experience, while also reflecting upon it.

In this writer's opinion, the learning-cycle approach offers a rich model for a civilization course, since it avoids presenting culture as a compilation of facts to be recited by instructors and memorized by students. It is conceived as a dynamic inquiry into the understanding of another culture, a progressive and never-ending apprenticeship in the acquisition of higher and measurable levels of cultural competence.

When successfully designed, a learning cycle will not only introduce students to new concepts, but also encourage them to reflect critically and provide them with a method to learn more on a given topic beyond the classroom framework. How these results can be obtained will be demonstrated with the example of a learning cycle prepared for a Contemporary French Civilization class, one centered on the theme of the French family.

The French Family: A Learning-Cycle Approach

Selection of a Topic

Since encouraging students' active participation is at the core of the learning-cycle strategy, the selection of a topic is best made in consultation with the students, perhaps from a list of topics established earlier in class. Instructors who like to retain more control over the topics to be covered in the course can provide the students with the chance to choose only the order in which suggested topics will be presented. In the following case, we will assume that the students choose to study the family in France.

Exploration

In this first stage, students recall and share concrete experiences they have had that relate to the topic. Since very few students will have had first-hand knowledge of the family in France, they will discuss an experience shared by all: the American family.

The focus of this phase can be clarified with a few specific directions such as: Prepare a brief for a foreign visitor on the topic; or, Write the table of contents for a book on the topic. This inventory of experiences is best done in small groups with minimal intervention on the part of the instructor. This interaction is in the target language, thus providing an opportunity for the students to familiarize themselves with needed vocabulary. The instructor's role during this exercise is not to be restricted to the role of linguistic informant, and much effort will be devoted to encouraging everyone's participation. Discussion can be stimulated and broadened with questions such as: Do you know of any statistics that can be relevant to this topic? What image of the family is given in the media? What reality does the Hollywood pattern of five or six successive marriages and divorces have? How does the legal system affect the institution of the family?

When the groups finish their inventory, the instructor acts as secretary, putting on the board every item reported as significant by each group of informants. There are no efforts to classify these experiences and observations at this point and sources are not discussed.

Invention

This phase can be divided into two periods:

Data Analysis.   Faced with an accumulation of data on the board, students are asked to sort through them. Some tasks are obvious, and repeated items can be deleted. Some items are more complex and can be arranged under general headings: family and government, work and family, the makeup of the family unit, etc. What to do with conflicting data must also be decided. This last point leads naturally to the question of sources: Did the students learn what they know through personal experience? through the media? If so, what kind of medium?

The instructor intervenes with questions formulated to focus the students' attention on aspects of the family that may have been overlooked. One may wish to discuss the role played by older family members or the effect of the ever-increasing number of women working outside the home; the support given to the institution by special legislation may also be examined. All new information resulting from these discussions is filed under a proper heading.

At the end of this phase, students not only will have created a document illustrating the concept of family in the United States, but also will be able to explain how the document was created, to quote its sources, and to recognize its strengths and weaknesses.

Invention.   After having collected data through sharing experiences and analyzing and evaluating them, students are now asked what data and information they need in order to understand the French concept of what a family is. Reflecting on the type of work they did earlier, they are to choose and decide, indeed "invent," the types of information they need to gather, from what sources and in what sequence. In order to encourage a very broad perspective, students should be encouraged to explore aspects of the topic they prefer. Some students may want to gather statistics, others may want to read scholarly articles, while still others may prefer to leaf through the daily and weekly press. Some will want to share their personal experiences: observations or knowledge gained through literature, films, and TV shows. A few students may want to explore stereotypes they are curious about: strict French fathers, ménage à trois, etc., while others will be interested in studying government policies and the laws protecting the family.

Once again the instructor writes on the board students' suggestions about what aspects of the topic they want to research. These suggestions are organized and prioritized: during this "invention" stage, the need for specific information is defined and a method to gather this information is "invented."

The instructor should now give sources for information that the students are interested in. Each student or group of students is then assigned a very precise task to accomplish for the next class meeting: read an article or a statistical study, make a list of the laws affecting the family existence, watch an excerpt of French TV, with the goal of reporting findings to the whole class during the application phase.

Application

First, individuals or groups give short reports in the sequence determined during the invention phase. Whenever conflicting evidence has been gathered (and the instructor will have taken care to include conflicting materials!), students will be encouraged to reach a compromise: at the very least, the fact that all sources of information do not coincide must be reported. All reports, once presented, discussed, and possibly amended in class, will be reproduced and distributed. Everyone will thus receive a file on the topic researched. The instructor should stress that this file is not a definitive study but rather a departure point to be built upon and revised according to availability of data. Concrete suggestions may be given for additional readings and activities (watch a film, interview a campus personality), if more information is wanted by individuals on a particular aspect of the topic.

Contrastive Analysis *Only* after Learning Cycle

At this point, and only at this point, can contrastive analysis have a chance to be successful. Because students have researched and given thought to the concept of family in *both* American and French society, they are now able to make comparisons and venture educated guesses about why the resemblances and differences are as they are.

In order to experiment successfully with a learning cycle, all of the steps must be observed for the following reasons:

1. The *exploration* not only provides students with a chance to list and articulate their previous experiences, but also, through sharing with the group, introduces them to new sets of concrete experiences.

2. The *invention* phase starts with an analysis of the exploration phase and an assessment of its results. Reflecting on the nature of these results and the manner in which they were obtained, students are asked to determine if this same approach can be applied to research the topic at hand, if it can be improved, and if so, how? Their answers to these questions will determine an appropriate method to process information subsequently made available to them.

3. The *application* phase provides further experience that will broaden and stabilize the knowledge acquired in researching the topic suggested.

Adopting a learning-cycle approach in the civilization course is not an easy decision to make. Some faculty members are uncomfortable with a method that requires students' active participation in the learning process. For those who prefer *lecturing to* rather than *listening to* their students, the learning-cycle approach would appear to be a time-consuming, difficult, and inefficient way to educate.

Resistance to the learning cycle also initiates with students who, lacking confidence in themselves or fellow students, prefer to have the instructor be their sole source of knowledge. This initial resistance should be expected and is quickly overcome once the students are encouraged to take more initiative.

Creating a learning cycle requires much behind-the-scenes work on the part of the instructor, since there appears to be no fixed agenda. In particular, a great deal of thought should be given to question preparation. Students should be stimulated, without being intimidated, to examine aspects of the topic that did not come up spontaneously.

It is important that the instructors have on hand substantial documentation relevant to the topic. Students are to process all materials themselves instead of having it done for them, as is often the case in a traditional lecture. There are also textbooks that offer a wealth of varied materials from which it is possible to build a learning cycle (Paoletti and Steele, 13).

The way students are evaluated must also fit the learning-cycle approach. Mechanical means of testing, such as true/false or multiple-choice questions, are abandoned. A more creative approach, which requires reflection rather than memorization, is needed. A good example of this would be to place in context a short press clipping treating one aspect of the topic researched. Students can also be encouraged to challenge (or ratify) claims made by the media. Items such as a carefully chosen cartoon, an advertisement, or a short scene from a film lend themselves to becoming worthy examination questions when students are asked to note all relevant connotations.

Benefits of the Learning-Cycle Approach

The amount of work required in preparing this type of class is readily justified by the benefits derived from the learning-cycle methodology.

1. In this learner-centered approach, students' knowledge and past experiences are not only acknowledged but credited to them. The class starts at a point (exploration) where it is possible for everyone to become involved; no one is starting completely from scratch—an encouraging feeling!

2. The learning cycle provides a concrete experiential basis for discussions of more abstract principles, wherein learning to think takes precedence over memorization, and the needs of students at different levels of their cognitive development are met. As pointed out by Karplus (11), students who use concrete reasoning patterns are not excluded from class participation, and the formation of formal reasoning patterns is made an ongoing part of the course.

3. The learning cycle is also an effective tool in fighting stereotyping, a prevalent danger in a culture class. Addressing a Cornell University audience in 1964, Piaget stated:

   > The great danger is of slogans, collective opinions, ready-made trends of thought. We have to be able to resist individually, to criticize, to distinguish between what is proven and what is not. So we need pupils who are *active*, who learn early *to find out* by themselves, partly *by their own spontaneous activity* and partly *through material we set up for them;* who learn early to tell what is verifiable and what is simply the first idea to come to them (reported in Duckworth, 6, p. 175; emphasis added).

   In sharing information and analyzing data critically, students have an opportunity to view a topic through the eyes of others. Being systematically offered a variety of information sources encourages reviewing data from different perspectives.

4. The learning-cycle approach is an effective way to fight instructor boredom. Since no two groups of students share exactly the same experiences and concerns, no learning cycle evolves in the same manner. Even for the most seasoned instructor, a certain degree of anticipation is forever present.

In the search for newer and better methodologies adaptable to the civilization course, the learning-cycle approach is an objective effort borrowed from the sciences and applied to a field often considered highly subjective, the study of culture. Its most obvious benefit is greater involvement in the learning process and, thus, better retention of knowledge gained by incorporating the formation of reasoning patterns and providing interaction. Ability to interact is essential to cultural competency and must be practiced in the classroom.

References

1. *ACTFL Provisional Proficiency Guidelines*. Hastings-on-Hudson, NY: ACTFL Materials Center, 1982.

2. Allen, Wendy. "Toward Cultural Proficiency," pp. 137-66 in Alice C. Omaggio, ed., *Proficiency, Curriculum, Articulation: The Ties That Bind*. Middlebury, VT: The Northeast Conference, 1985.

3. Brière, Jean-François. "Cultural Understanding through Cross Cultural Analysis." *The French Review* 60 (1986):203-8.

4. Carr, Thomas. "Contemporary Culture: A Model for Teaching a Culture's Heritage," pp. 71-83 in P. Westphal, ed., *Meeting the Call for Excellence in the Foreign Language Classroom*. Report of Central States Conference on the Teaching of Foreign Languages. Lincolnwood, IL: National Textbook Company, 1985.

5. Debyser, Francis. "Lecture des civilisations," pp. 9-17 in Beacco et Lieutaud, *Mœurs et Mythes*. Paris: Hachette/Larousse, 1981.

6. Duckworth, Eleanore. "Piaget Rediscovered." *Journal of Research in Science Teaching* 2 (1964):172-75.

7. ETS Oral Proficiency Testing Manual. Princeton, NJ: Educational Testing Service, 1982.

8. Fuller, Robert, et al. *Piagetian Programs in Higher Education*. University of Nebraska–Lincoln, ADAPT, 1981.

9. Inhelder, Barbel, and Jean Piaget. *The Growth of Logical Thinking from Childhood to Adolescence*. New York: Basic Books, 1958.

10. Karplus, Robert. *Science Curriculum Improvement Study*. Berkeley, CA: University of California, 1974.

11. _____. "Science Teaching and the Development of Reasoning." *Journal of Research in Science Teaching* 14 (1977):169-75.

12. Knox, Edward. "À Propos de compétence culturelle," pp. 99-100 in L. Porcher, ed., *La Civilisation*. Paris: Clé International, 1981.

13. Paoletti, Michel, et Ross Steele. *La Civilisation française quotidienne*. Nouvelle édition. Paris: Hatier, 1986.

14. Perry, William. *Forms of Intellectual and Ethical Development in the College Years: A Scheme*. New York: Holt, Rinehart and Winston, 1968.

Central States Conference Proceedings

Published annually in conjunction with the
Central States Conference on the Teaching of Foreign Languages

For further information or a current catalog, write:
National Textbook Company
a division of *NTC Publishing Group*
4255 West Touhy Avenue
Lincolnwood, Illinois 60646-1975 U.S.A.